Fish Species
of New Zealand

A PHOTOGRAPHIC GUIDE

Jorge Hirt-Chabbert

This guide is dedicated to my parents,
Dora and Kurt.

A RAUPO BOOK
Published by the Penguin Group
Penguin Group (NZ), 67 Apollo Drive, Rosedale,
North Shore 0632, New Zealand (a division of Pearson New Zealand Ltd)
Penguin Group (USA) Inc., 375 Hudson Street,
New York, New York 10014, USA
Penguin Group (Canada), 90 Eglinton Avenue East, Suite 700, Toronto,
Ontario, M4P 2Y3, Canada (a division of Pearson Penguin Canada Inc.)
Penguin Books Ltd, 80 Strand, London, WC2R 0RL, England
Penguin Ireland, 25 St Stephen's Green,
Dublin 2, Ireland (a division of Penguin Books Ltd)
Penguin Group (Australia), 250 Camberwell Road, Camberwell,
Victoria 3124, Australia (a division of Pearson Australia Group Pty Ltd)
Penguin Books India Pvt Ltd, 11, Community Centre,
Panchsheel Park, New Delhi – 110 017, India
Penguin Books (South Africa) (Pty) Ltd, 24 Sturdee Avenue,
Rosebank, Johannesburg 2196, South Africa

Penguin Books Ltd, Registered Offices: 80 Strand, London, WC2R 0RL, England

Originally published by Reed Publishing (NZ) Ltd 2006
First published by Penguin Group (NZ), 2008
1 3 5 7 9 10 8 6 4 2

Copyright © Jorge Hirt-Chabbert, 2006

The right of Jorge Hirt-Chabbert to be identified as the author of this work in terms of
section 96 of the Copyright Act 1994 is hereby asserted.

Printed in China through Bookbuilders, Hong Kong

All rights reserved. Without limiting the rights under copyright reserved above,
no part of this publication may be reproduced, stored in or introduced into a retrieval
system, or transmitted, in any form or by any means (electronic, mechanical,
photocopying, recording or otherwise), without the prior written permission of
both the copyright owner and the above publisher of this book.

ISBN: 978 0 14 301095 1

A catalogue record for this book is available
from the National Library of New Zealand.

www.penguin.co.nz

Disclaimer
The author and publisher do not warrant that the information contained in this book is free from errors
or omissions. All care has been taken to ensure all information provided is correct and as current as
possible at time of first publication.

Contents

Introduction	5
How to use this guide	5
ID card	6
Fish body descriptions	8
The continental shelf and slope	10
Glossary	11
Cartilaginous fishes	**13**
Bony fishes	**31**
References	128
Index of common names	130
Index of scientific names	132

Introduction

This book is a consequence of the need for a comprehensive and easy-to-use identification guide to New Zealand seafood species. Included are 110 marine finfish species or fish species group. The selection of these species was made on the basis of almost daily observation of seafood on board vessels, in factories and in fish shops throughout New Zealand over a period of six years.

All images in the book have been taken by the author and are of fresh specimens, and, without losing scientific rigour, the text has been written as simply as possible. Many species of fish can be recognised using only the image as a general reference in terms of appearance facets such as coloration and shape. Those features that are easy to check have been prioritised and technical terms have been avoided as much as possible.

These external features are complemented with information about the average length, weight, distribution and spawning seasons for each species. This information is the result of extensive data research from many sources as well as from direct observation. The author recognises that contradictions do exist among the different sources of information and that better data are needed for many species.

How to use this guide

Each seafood species is presented in the form of an 'identification card' (see pages 6–7), and includes concise information about the fish for rapid identification. Each entry includes a brief list of the most important diagnostic identification characteristics for the fish, accompanied by easy-to-check features that will help distinguish the species from other similar fish.

Technical terms have been avoided as much as possible. However, in order to present the information about the fish in a scientifically correct manner, it is helpful that the reader has some comprehension of technical terminology to aid correct identification. The fish body descriptions on pages 8 and 9, the information on sea zones on page 10 and the glossary on pages 11 and 12 are designed to give the reader the technological knowledge required to fully utilise the information in this book.

The order of species has been arranged using a taxonomic sequence, commencing with sharks and rays and ending with the leatherjacket and the moonfish; the same sequence as used in *New Zealand Fishes* by Larry Paul. This order allows the grouping of similar species near each other so a quick scan can be made of similar fishes.

The information for a particular species or group can be found by visually inspecting the imagery or by using the index of common names on page 130 or the index of scientific names on page 132.

Common name (1) *Scientific name (2)*

Maori name (3)

Identification features (4)

Ruler (5)

Identification features (4)

Length (6)
Weight (7)

Distribution in the water column (9)
Depth range (10)
Spawning season (11)

Similar common species (12)

Distribution map (8)

ID card

1. **Common name:** The most widely accepted New Zealand common name.

2. *Scientific name:* The most recent scientific name, although it must be noted revision may occur.

3. **Maori name:** if in general use.

4. **Identification features:** The most important diagnostic identification characteristics of the species or species group. The characteristics in bold are external features that are easy to check, and are useful for quick identification against similar common species.

5. **Ruler:** Included to give a general idea of fish size.

6. **Length:** This is the average length range for the species. The upper number is the largest recorded size in literature available.

7. **Weight:** This is the average weight range for the species. The upper number is the largest recorded weight in literature available.

8. **Distribution map:** Shading touching the coastline represents a distribution over the continental shelf, or the continental shelf and slope. Shading separated from the coastline indicates species distributed on the continental slope only.

9. **Distribution in the water column:** Either over the continental shelf and/or the continental slope. Indicates whether species are demersal, semi-pelagic or pelagic.

10. **Depth range:** Gives the full range and the most common range of the species.

11. **Spawning season:** Gives the time for spawning for each species.

12. **Similar common species:** These are commonly caught species that are similar in appearance to the entry you are looking at, but are not necessarily related.

Note: in some instances particular information about a species is unavailable at the time of writing this book.

Fish body descriptions

Body features of a shark

Body features of a bony fish

The continental shelf and slope

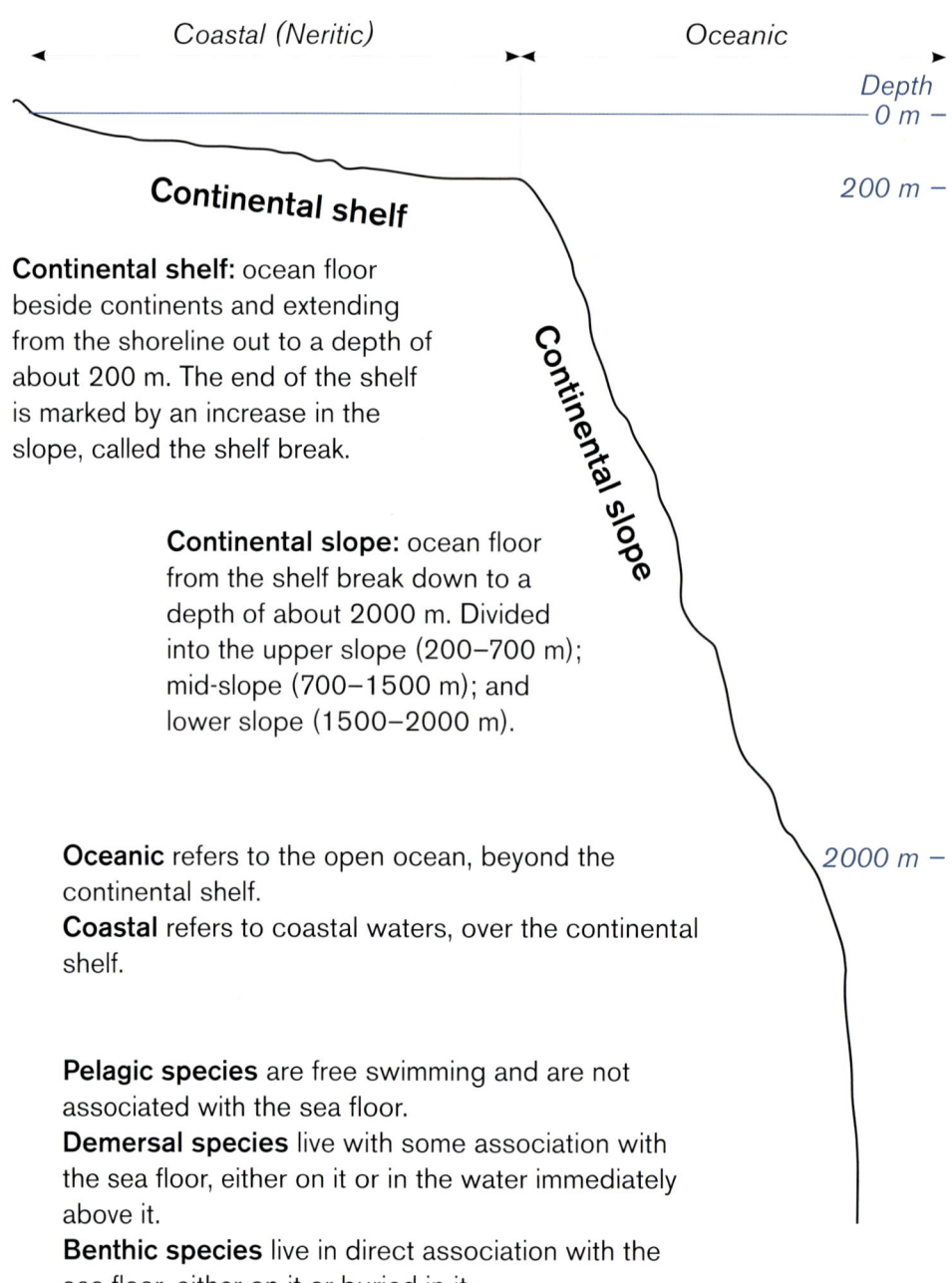

Continental shelf: ocean floor beside continents and extending from the shoreline out to a depth of about 200 m. The end of the shelf is marked by an increase in the slope, called the shelf break.

Continental slope: ocean floor from the shelf break down to a depth of about 2000 m. Divided into the upper slope (200–700 m); mid-slope (700–1500 m); and lower slope (1500–2000 m).

Oceanic refers to the open ocean, beyond the continental shelf.
Coastal refers to coastal waters, over the continental shelf.

Pelagic species are free swimming and are not associated with the sea floor.
Demersal species live with some association with the sea floor, either on it or in the water immediately above it.
Benthic species live in direct association with the sea floor, either on it or buried in it.

Glossary

Adipose fin A small fleshy fin without rays, found on the back behind the dorsal fin of some fishes, for example, silversides.

Anal fin The median, unpaired, ventrally located fin that lies behind the anus, usually on the posterior half of the fish.

Aplacental Not connected to female fish by a placenta.

Barbel Fleshy projection near the mouth, chin or snout as in catfish or cod; a slender tentacle-like protuberance, generally used for locating food.

Caudal fin The tail or tail fin. It may be rounded or square-tipped, slightly indented, or deeply forked.

Caudal peduncle The narrow part of the body between the posterior ends of the dorsal and anal fins and the base of the caudal fin.

Dorsal fin A median fin along the back that is supported by rays. There may be two or more dorsal fins; in these cases the most anterior one is designated the first dorsal fin.

Fin rays The supporting bony elements of fins, including spines and soft rays; all fin supports are rays whether segmented, unsegmented or spinous, but sometimes the term ray is used to denote soft rays only.

Finlets The small individual fins posterior to the second dorsal and anal fins, for example, in tuna.

Fins Folds of skin supported by cartilaginous tissue in cartilaginous fishes, and by bony rays in bony fishes. Used for locomotion and display. Sometimes have specialised functions such as fertilisation.

Free rear tip Posterior tip of a fin closest to the fin insertion.

Gill Respiratory organ of many aquatic animals; a filamentous outgrowth well supplied with blood vessels at which gas exchange between water and blood occurs.

Gill cover The bones of the head that cover the gill chamber; also called the operculum.

Gill opening An opening behind the head that connects the gill chamber to the exterior. Bony fishes have a single opening on each side; cartilaginous fishes (sharks and rays) have five to seven openings. The gill openings of sharks and rays are called gill slits.

Gill slits Gill openings in sharks and rays.

Interdorsal ridge Ridge of skin between the first and second dorsal fins.

Jaws Part of the mouth supporting the teeth.

Keel A lateral fleshy or bony ridge on the caudal peduncle or base of the caudal fin.

Lateral line A sensory organ of fishes that consists of a line of pores along the side of the body. Used to detect sounds and other disturbances in the water.

Lunate Sickle-shaped. Used to describe a caudal fin that is deeply emarginate with narrow lobes; shaped like a crescent moon.

Notch An indentation, usually in a fin, dividing it into two parts or lobes.

Oophagus Feeds on eggs.

Operculum Bony gill cover.

Origin The beginning; often used for the anterior end of the dorsal or anal fin at the base.

Pectoral fin The paired fins attached to the pectoral girdle.

Pelvic fin The paired fin that is located posterior, ventral or anterior to the pectoral fins (abdominal, thoracic or jugular in position).

Precaudal pit A transverse or longitudinal notch on the caudal peduncle just in front of the caudal fin of sharks. Also called the caudal pit.

Scale A small, membranous or horny, stiff, typically plate-like body in the skin of fishes, serving to protect, colour and support the body. May be modified into spines, tubercles, bony plates or an exoskeleton, reduced or even lost.

Scutes Hard, thick external plates derived from scales and present on the skin of some fishes, for example, Jack mackerels.

Snout The part of the head in front of the eye; the distance from the eye to the anterior tip of the head above the upper jaw (normally the upper lip).

Soft ray A segmented fin ray that is composed of two closely joined lateral elements. It is nearly always flexible and often branched.

Species A group of animals or plants having common characteristics. They are able to breed together to produce fertile offspring so that they maintain their 'separateness' from other groups; the basic rank of biological nomenclature. Taxonomically, the name of a category of organisms below the genus group. Abbreviated as sp. (singular) or spp. (plural).

Spine 1) A sharp projecting point; if referring to fins, a stiff unsegmented, undivided and unbranched element supporting and/or arming the fin. It is not laterally paired as in rays.

2) Sharp, hard bony structures on the skeleton or skin, for example, the preopercular spines.

Truncate With square ends; used to describe a caudal fin with a vertically straight terminal border and angular or slightly rounded corners; terminating abruptly, as in a cut-off square.

Viviparous When a female gives birth to live young, not eggs.

Wing The enlarged pectoral fins in rays and skates.

Cartilaginous fishes

Mako shark *Isurus oxyrinchus*

Maori name: Mako

Indigo-blue above, changing abruptly from blue on the flanks to white

Second dorsal fin origin in front of anal fin origin

One large keel on each side of the caudal peduncle

10 cm

Length: 200–300 cm, up to 400 cm (born at about 60–70 cm)
Weight: up to 450 kg

Similar common species

Porbeagle shark (p. 15)

A pelagic species, principally in the open ocean, but also over the continental shelf.
Depth range: 0–700 m, most common in 0–150 m.
Aplacental, producing litters of 4–18 pups. Oophagous.

Porbeagle shark *Lamna nasus*

Bluish-grey above, white below

Second dorsal fin origin over anal fin origin

Two keels on each side of the caudal peduncle

10 cm

Length: 150–250 cm, up to 350 cm (born at about 70–80 cm)
Weight: up to 280 kg

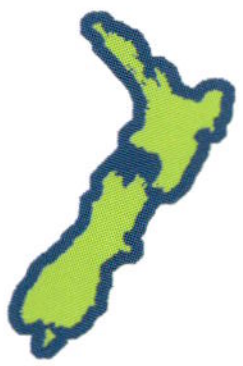

A pelagic species, principally in the open ocean, but also over the outer continental shelf.
Depth range: 0–700 m, most common in 0–300 m.
Aplacental viviparous, producing litters of 1–5 pups. Oophagous.

Similar common species

Mako shark (p. 14)

Blue shark *Prionace glauca*

Maori name: *Pounamu*

**Indigo-blue above, white below
Body fusiform, slender**

|—| 10 cm

Length: Around 200 cm, up to 380 cm
(born at about 35–50 cm)
Weight: up to 180 kg

A pelagic species, principally in the open ocean, but also over the continental shelf.
Depth range: 0–350 m.
Placental viviparous, producing litters of 4–135 pups (average about 40); born in spring and summer after 9–12 months' gestation.

Bronze whaler *Carcharhinus brachyurus*

Maori name: Horopekapeka

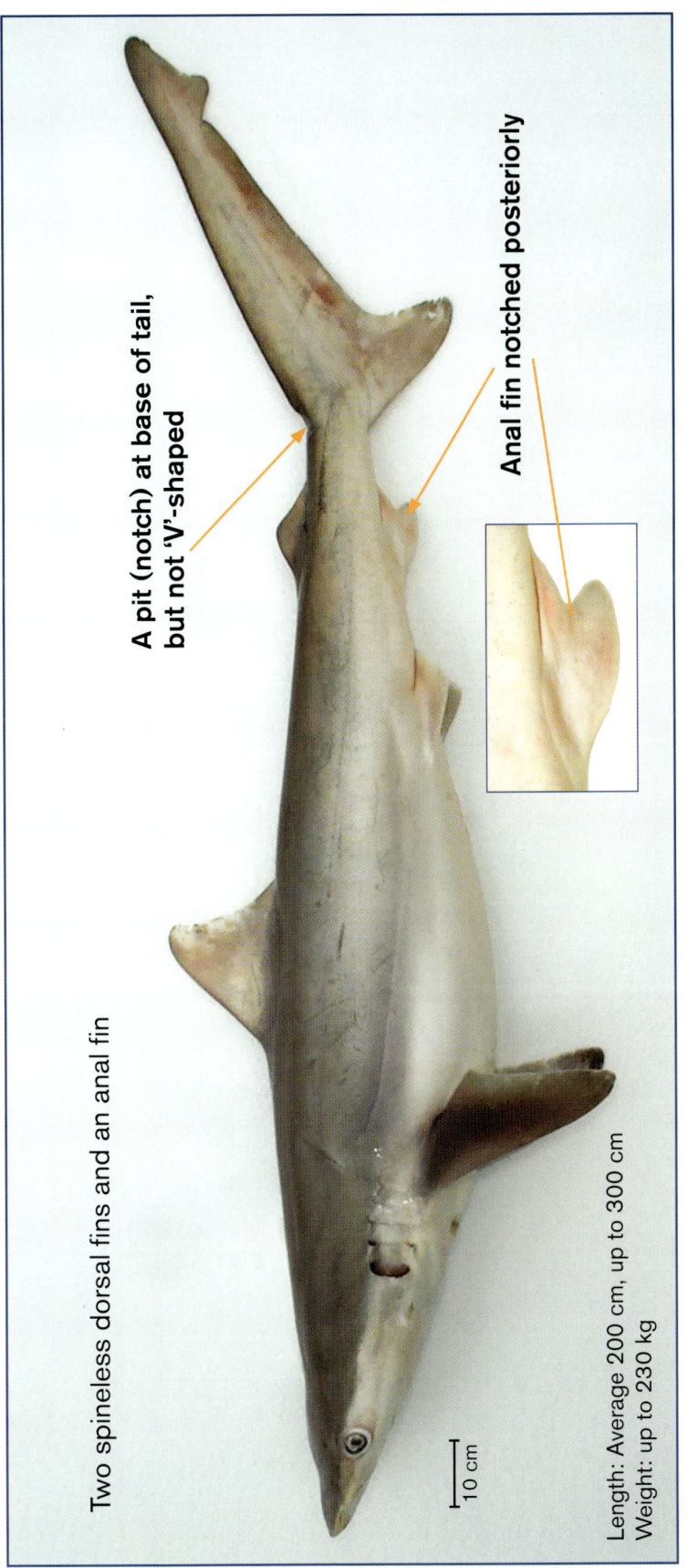

Two spineless dorsal fins and an anal fin

A pit (notch) at base of tail, but not 'V'-shaped

Anal fin notched posteriorly

Length: Average 200 cm, up to 300 cm
Weight: up to 230 kg

A mainly pelagic species over the inner continental shelf. Depth range: 0–100 m, most common in 0–50 m. Placental viviparous, producing litters of 7–20 pups; born in spring and early summer.

Similar common species

Hammerhead shark (p. 19)
(when head and tail removed)

School shark (p. 20)

Thresher shark *Alopias vulpinus*

Maori name: Mangoo-ripi

Tail very long, as long as rest of body

Blue-grey above, white below.
Irregular white patch on the flanks

10 cm

Length: 300–400 cm, up to 550 cm (born at about 115–150 cm)
Weight: up to 350 kg

A pelagic species over the continental shelf and on the open ocean. Young often close inshore.
Depth range: 0–550 m, most common in 0–300 m.
Aplacental viviparous, producing litters of 2–4 pups. Oophagous.

Hammerhead shark *Sphyrna zygaena*

Maori name: Mangoo-pare

- Head hammer-shaped
- A deep 'V'-shaped pit (notch) at base of tail
- Anal fin deeply notched posteriorly
- Two spineless dorsal fins and an anal fin

Length: Most specimens around New Zealand are juveniles of about 100 cm up to 350 cm (born at about 50–60 cm)
Weight: 3–15 kg (juveniles) up to 200 kg

A mainly pelagic species over the continental shelf. Depth range: 0–110 m, most common in 0–50 m. Placental viviparous, producing litters of 20–50 pups; born in summer after a gestation of 10–11 months.

Similar common species

Bronze whaler shark  (p. 17)
(when head and tail removed)

School shark  (p. 20)

School shark *Galeorhinus australis*

Maori name: Tupere

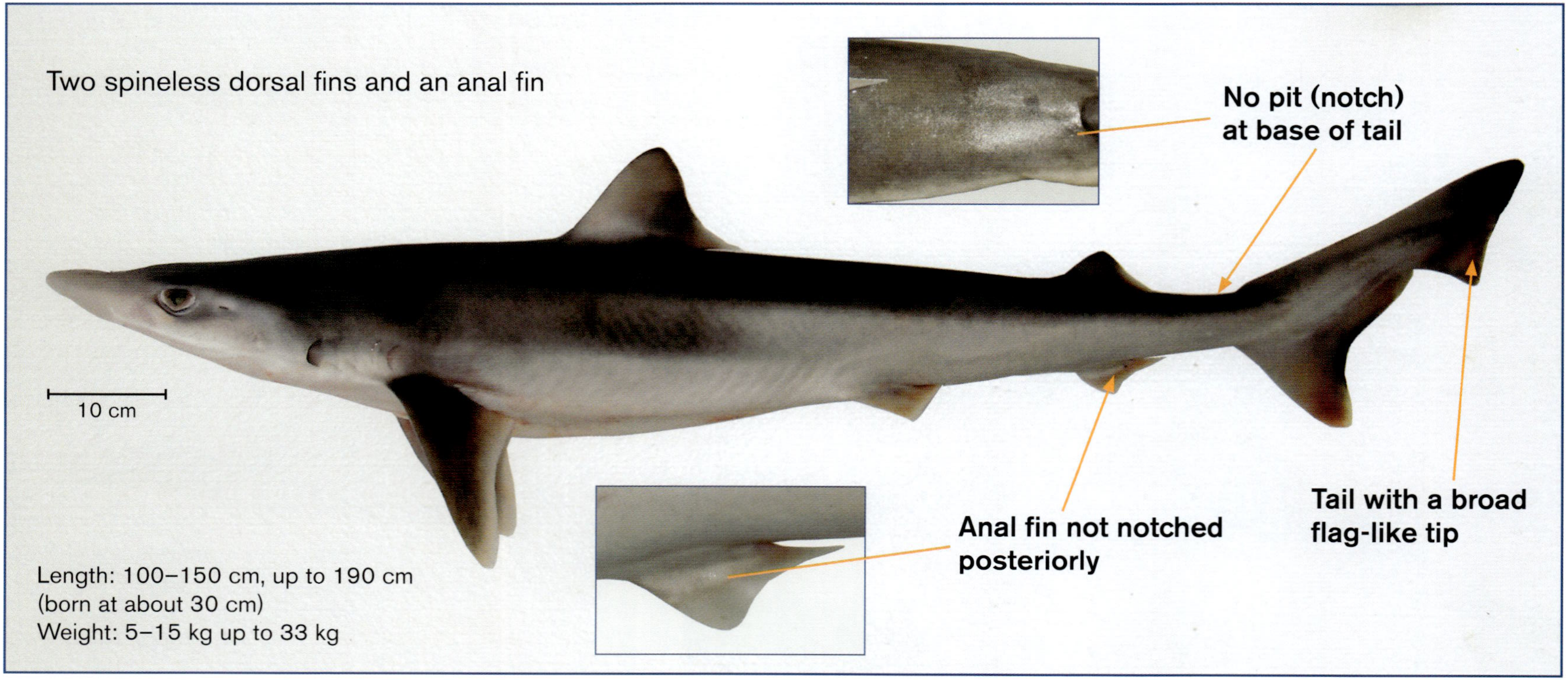

Two spineless dorsal fins and an anal fin

No pit (notch) at base of tail

Tail with a broad flag-like tip

Anal fin not notched posteriorly

Length: 100–150 cm, up to 190 cm (born at about 30 cm)
Weight: 5–15 kg up to 33 kg

10 cm

Mainly a demersal species over the continental shelf, but they are also pelagic in the open ocean. Depth range: 0–500 m, most common in 0–200 m. Aplacental viviparous, producing litters of 15–43 pups, born in spring and summer after a gestation of 12 months. Young sharks use bays and estuaries as nursery areas.

Similar common species

Bronze whaler shark (p. 17)
Hammerhead shark (p. 19)
(when head and tail removed)

Rig *Mustelus lenticulatus*

Two spineless dorsal fins and an anal fin
Interdorsal ridge present

Golden brown above with many small white spots, white below

Second dorsal fin bigger than anal fin

Length: 70–100 cm, up to 140 cm (born at about 30–35 cm)
Weight: 2–5 kg

A near-bottom species over the continental shelf.
Depth range: 0–200 m, most common in 0–50 m.
Aplacental viviparous, producing litters of 2–23 pups, born in summer after a gestation of about 12 months.

Spiny dogfish *Squalus acanthias*

Maori name: Koinga

Brownish-grey above with a few diffuse white spots, white below

Dorsal fins with strong spines

Anal fin absent

Origin of first dorsal fin behind free rear tips of pectoral fin

10 cm

Length: 60–100 cm, up to 120 cm (born at about 18–30 cm)
Weight: usually 2–5 kg

A demersal and pelagic species over the continental shelf and upper slope. Depth range: 0–800 m, most common in 50–500 m. Aplacental viviparous, producing litters of 1–20 pups, born after a gestation of 18–24 months. It has the longest gestation known of all sharks.

Similar common species

Northern spiny dogfish (p. 23)

Northern spiny dogfish *Squalus mitsukuri*

Grey above, paler below
No white spots

Dorsal fins with strong spines

Origin of first dorsal fin over free rear tips of pectoral fin

Anal fin absent

10 cm

Length: 60–90 cm, up to 110 cm (born at about 22 cm)
Weight: 2–5 kg

A demersal species over the outer continental shelf and upper slope.
Depth range: 100–600 m, most common in 150–200 m.
Aplacental viviparous, producing litters of 4–9 pups.

Similar common species

Spiny dogfish (p. 22)

23

Rough skate *Dipturus nasutus*

Maori name: Uku

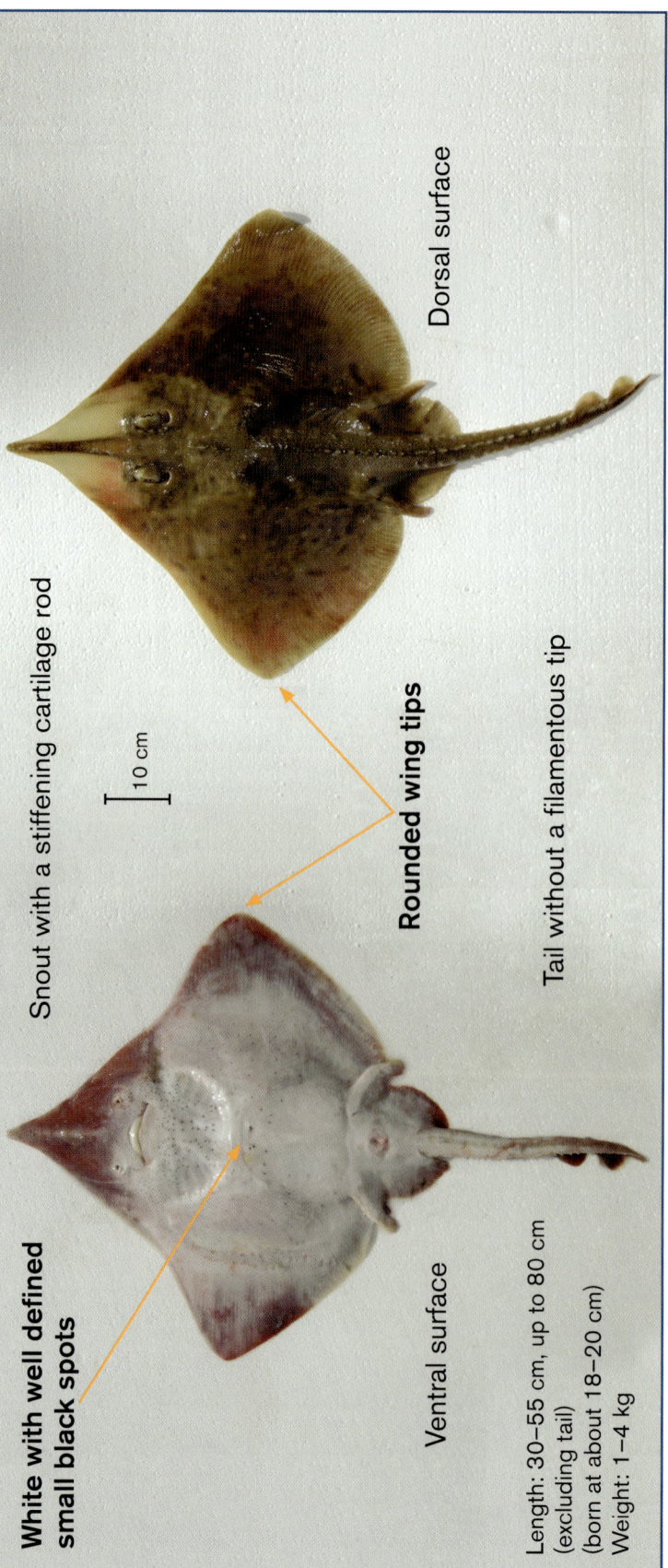

White with well defined small black spots

Snout with a stiffening cartilage rod

Rounded wing tips

Tail without a filamentous tip

Dorsal surface

Ventral surface

Length: 30–55 cm, up to 80 cm (excluding tail)
(born at about 18–20 cm)
Weight: 1–4 kg

A demersal species over the continental shelf and upper slope.
Depth range: 10–500 m.
Oviparous. Females lay egg cases on the sea floor.

Similar common species

Smooth skate  (p. 25)

Eagle ray  (p. 26)

Smooth skate *Dipturus innominata*

Maori name: Uku

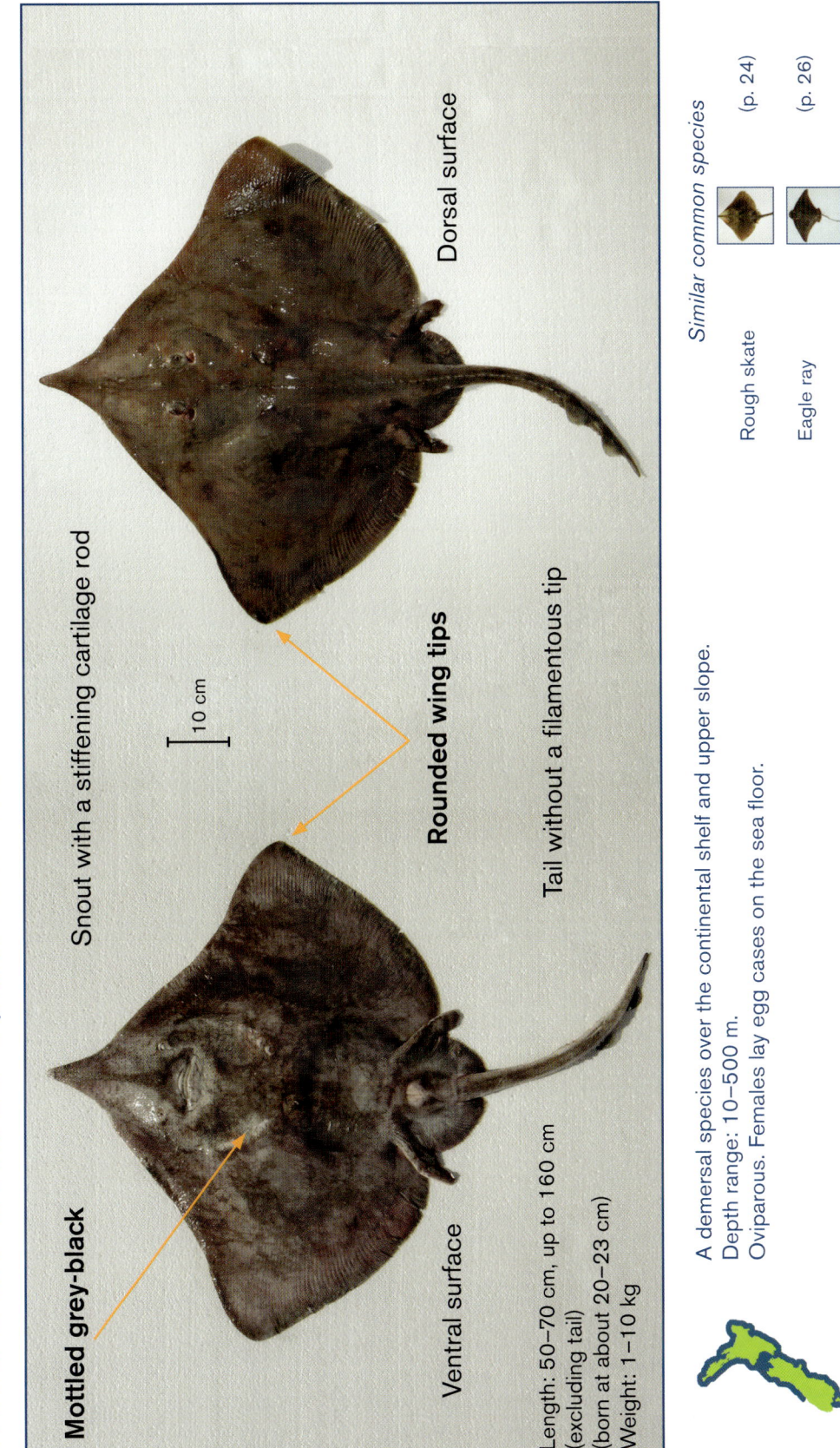

Mottled grey-black

Snout with a stiffening cartilage rod

Dorsal surface

Rounded wing tips

Ventral surface

Tail without a filamentous tip

10 cm

Length: 50–70 cm, up to 160 cm (excluding tail)
(born at about 20–23 cm)
Weight: 1–10 kg

A demersal species over the continental shelf and upper slope.
Depth range: 10–500 m.
Oviparous. Females lay egg cases on the sea floor.

Similar common species

Rough skate (p. 24)
Eagle ray (p. 26)

Eagle ray *Myliobatis tenuicaudatus*

Maori name: Whaikeo

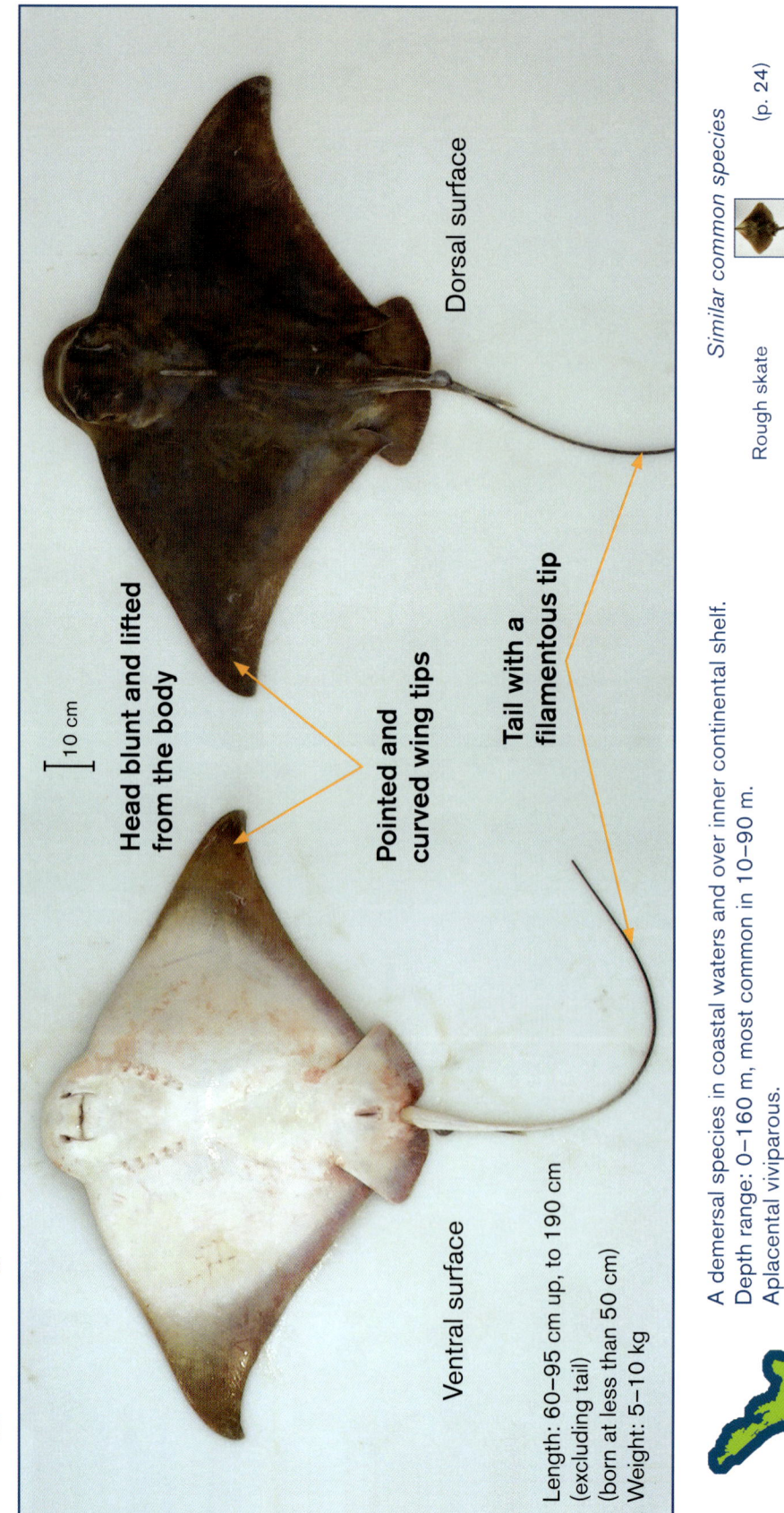

Dorsal surface

Head blunt and lifted from the body

Pointed and curved wing tips

Tail with a filamentous tip

Ventral surface

10 cm

Length: 60–95 cm up, to 190 cm (excluding tail)
(born at less than 50 cm)
Weight: 5–10 kg

A demersal species in coastal waters and over inner continental shelf.
Depth range: 0–160 m, most common in 10–90 m.
Aplacental viviparous.

Similar common species

Rough skate (p. 24)

Smooth skate (p. 25)

Elephantfish *Callorhinchus milii*

Maori name: Reperepe

- Hoe-shaped snout
- Short second dorsal fin
- Tail without a filamentous tip

10 cm

Length: 60–90 cm up, to 120 cm (born at about 15 cm)
Weight: 2–6 kg up to 9 kg

A bottom-dwelling species on the continental shelf.
Depth range: 0–200 m.
Oviparous. In spring and summer female migrate inshore to lay two eggs. Eggs encased in olive-brown capsules (about 25 cm long).

Similar common species

Pale ghost shark (p. 29)
Dark ghost shark (p. 28)

Dark ghost shark *Hydrolagus novaezelandiae*

Dark grey with white stripes and mottling above, silvery below

Second dorsal fin long and low

Anal fin absent

Long filament

Length: 50–60 cm up to 100 cm (without tail filament) (born at about 9–12 cm)
Weight: 0.6–3 kg

A demersal species over the outer continental shelf and upper slope. Depth range: 50–900 m, most common in 100–500 m. Oviparous. Females lay egg cases (spindle-like) on the sea floor.

Similar common species

Elephantfish (p. 27)

Pale ghost shark (p. 29)

Pale ghost shark *Hydrolagus* sp.

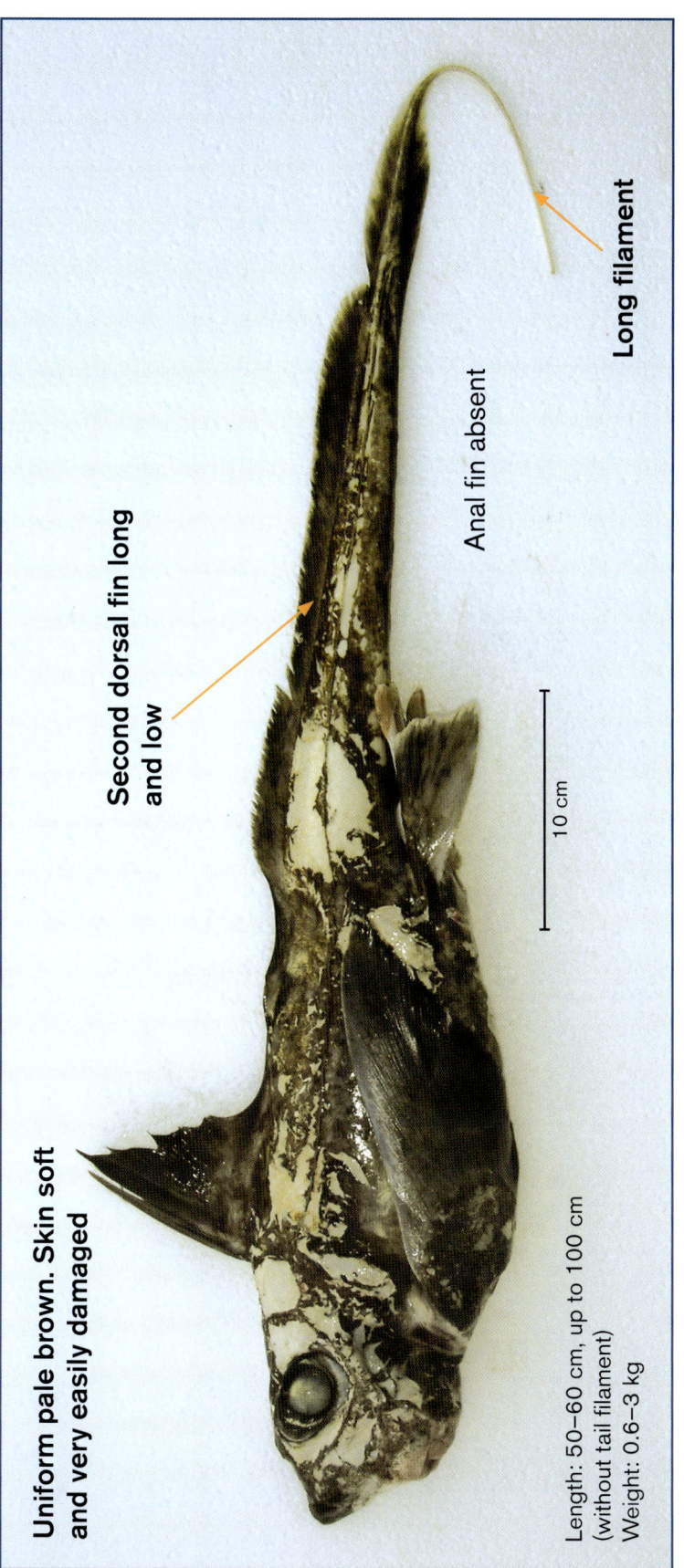

Uniform pale brown. Skin soft and very easily damaged

Second dorsal fin long and low

Anal fin absent

Long filament

10 cm

Length: 50–60 cm, up to 100 cm (without tail filament)
Weight: 0.6–3 kg

A demersal species over the continental slope.
Depth range: 400–800 m.
Oviparous. Females lay egg cases (spindle-like) on the sea floor.

Similar common species

Elephantfish (p. 27)

Dark ghost shark (p. 28)

Bony fishes

Pilchard *Sardinops neopilchardus*

Maori name: Mohimohi

Dark spots along the sides

Pelvic fin behind dorsal fin origin

10 cm

Length: 15–20 cm, up to 23 cm
Weight: less than 0.1 kg

A pelagic species over the continental shelf.
Depth range: 0–50 m.
Spawning occurs all year round in the north and during spring and summer in the south.

Similar common species

Sprats (p. 33)

Anchovy (p. 34)

Sprats *Sprattus antipodum; Sprattus muelleri*

Maori name: Kuupae

Pelvic fin below dorsal fin origin

Belly with serrated scales

Length: 8–12 cm, up to 15 cm
Weight: less than 0.1 kg

10 cm

Similar common species

Pilchard (p. 32)

Anchovy (p. 34)

A pelagic species over the continental shelf.
Depth range: 0–110 m, most common in 0–50 m.

33

Anchovy *Engraulis australis*

Maori name: Kokowhaawhaa

Snout in front of mouth

Mouth very large, end of jaw extending well past eye

Length: 8–12 cm, up to 16 cm
Weight: less than 0.1 kg

10 cm

A pelagic species over the continental shelf.
Depth range: 0–100 m.

Similar common species

Pilchard  (p. 32)

Sprats  (p. 33)

Conger eels *Conger verreauxi* (Common conger eel); *Conger wilsoni* (Northern conger eel)
Maori name: Ngoiro (Common conger eel); Kooiro (Northern conger eel)

Colour dark blue-grey to black
Skin thick and smooth, scales absent

Dorsal fin: origin above the pectoral tip (*C. verreauxi*) or behind the pectoral tip (*C. wilsoni*)

Pelvic fin absent

Pectoral fin well developed

Length: *C. verreauxi*: 100–150 cm, up to 220 cm; *C. wilsoni*: 70–80 cm, up to 100 cm;
Weight: 3–6 kg

A benthic species over the continental shelf, mostly solitary. Depth range: 0–50 m (*C. verreauxi*), 0–200 m (*C. wilsoni*). Breeding conger eels migrate to a ground well north of New Zealand and probably die after spawning.

Common conger eel   Northern conger eel

Silverside — *Argentina elongata*

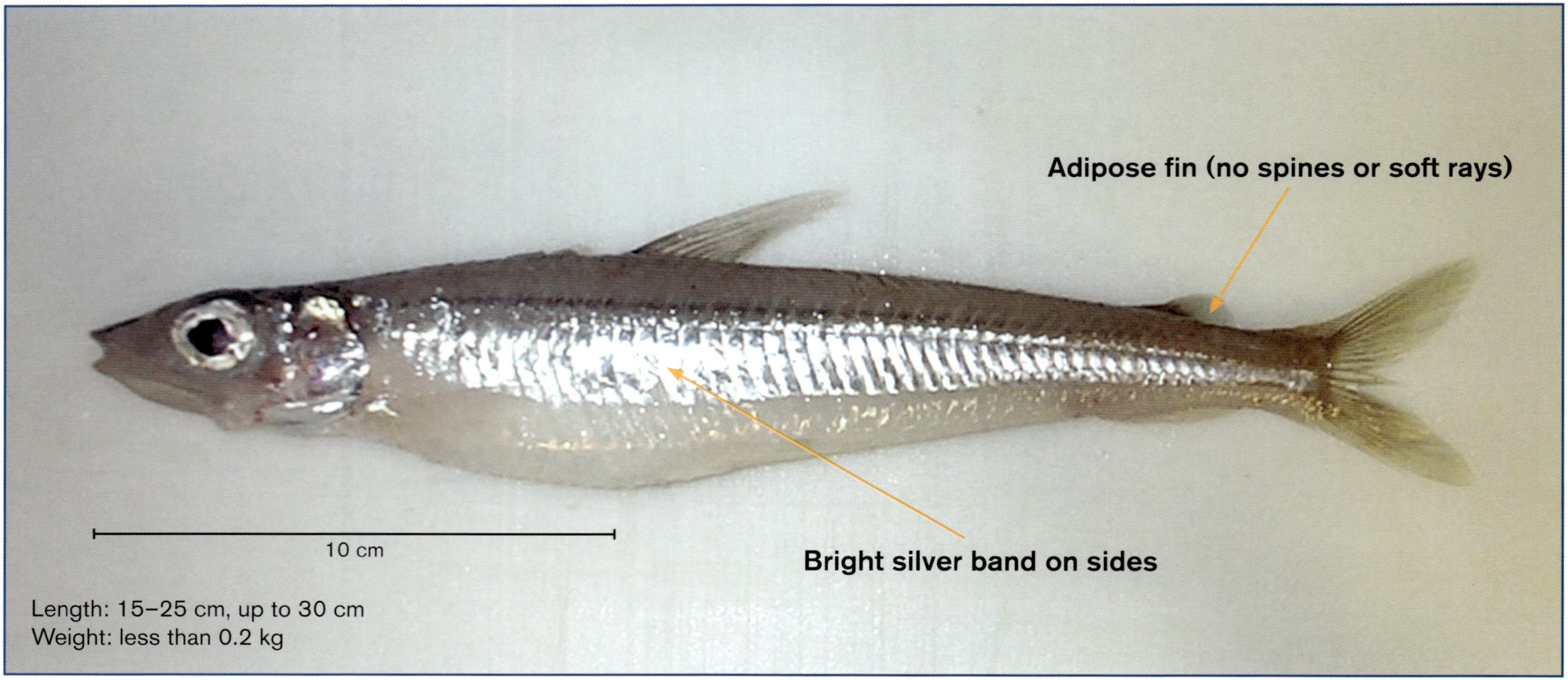

Adipose fin (no spines or soft rays)

Bright silver band on sides

10 cm

Length: 15–25 cm, up to 30 cm
Weight: less than 0.2 kg

A demersal species over the continental shelf and upper slope.
Depth range: 100–600 m.

Black cardinal *Epigonus telescopus*

Dark brown body
Large eye

Large and loose scales

10 cm

Length: 40–60 cm, up to 70 cm
Weight: 0.8–2.5 kg, up to 3 kg

A demersal species over the continental slope.
Depth range: 400–1000 m, most common in 700–900 m.

Southern blue whiting *Micromesistius australis*

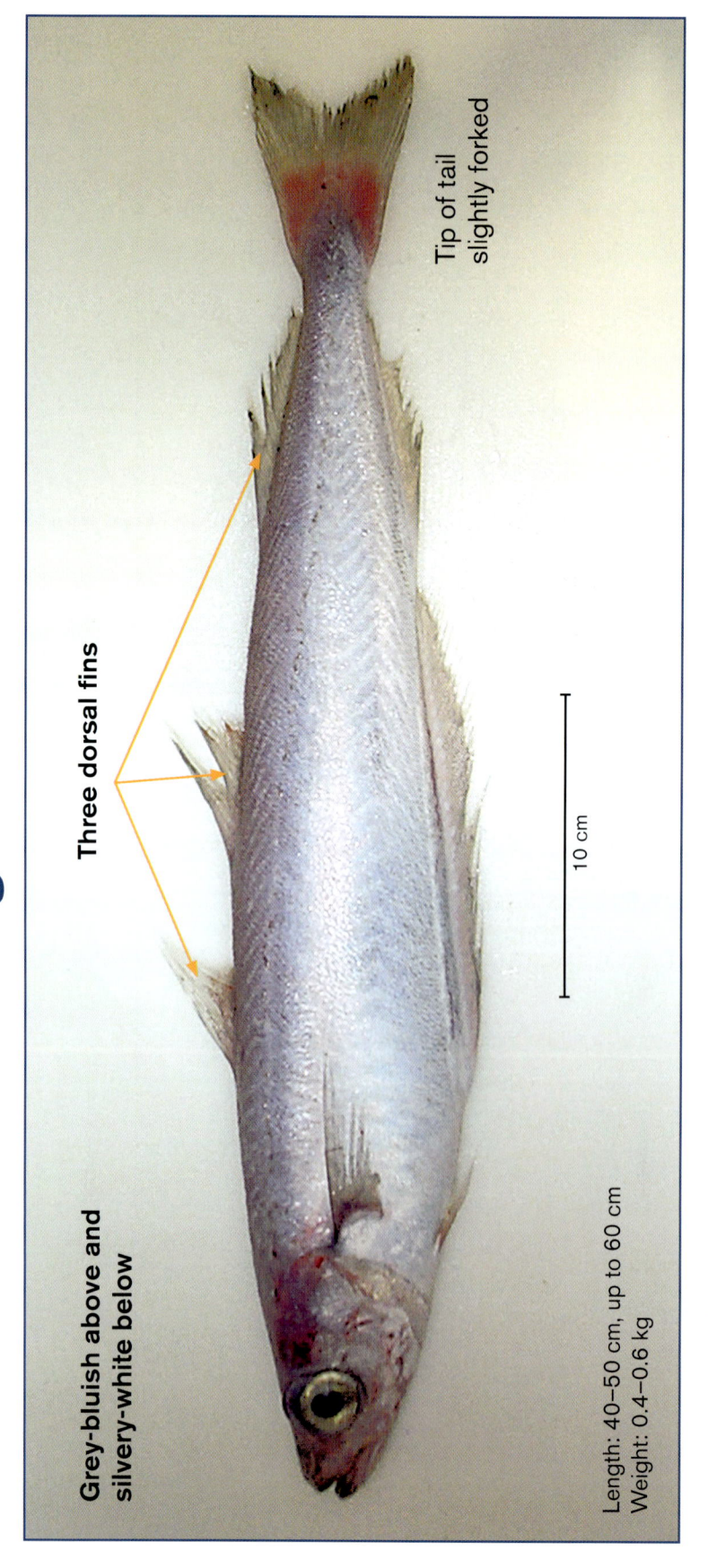

Grey-bluish above and silvery-white below

Three dorsal fins

Tip of tail slightly forked

10 cm

Length: 40–50 cm, up to 60 cm
Weight: 0.4–0.6 kg

Mainly a demersal species over the continental slope. Depth range: 300–700 m, most common in 450–650 m. Spawning occurs in spring.

Red cod *Pseudophycis bachus*

Maori name: Hoka

Second dorsal and anal fins: uniform in height
Scales above lateral line: 7–9

Tip of tail square

Black spot on pectoral fin base

Barbel: well developed

Length: 40–60 cm, up to 80 cm
Weight: 0.8–1.3 kg, up to 2.0 kg

10 cm

A demersal species on the continental shelf and upper slope.
Depth range: 10–700 m, most common in 100–300 m.
Spawning occurs in deep water during late winter and in spring.

Similar common species

Southern bastard cod (p. 40)

39

Southern bastard cod *Pseudophycis barbata*

Tip of tail rounded

Second dorsal and anal fins: uniform in height
Scales above lateral line: 13/16

10 cm

No black spot on pectoral fin base

Barbel: well developed

Length: 20–40 cm, up to 60 cm
Weight: 0.8–1.3 kg, up to 2.0 kg

A demersal species over the continental shelf.
Depth range: 10–250 m.
Spawning occurs during summer.

Similar common species

Red cod (p. 39)

Ribaldo *Mora moro*

Pale greyish to whitish

Large eye

First dorsal fin without long filament

Body soft, with very loose scales

Caudal fin slightly forked

Anal fin deeply notched (may appear as two fins)

Barbel: short

Length: 40–50 cm, up to 80 cm
Weight: 2–5 kg

10 cm

A demersal species over the continental slope.
Depth range: 300–1200 m, most common in 500–900 m.

Hake *Merluccius australis*

Maori name: Tiikati

Silvery-grey above, white below

- Tip of tail square
- Dorsal fin: two
- Second dorsal fin and anal fin deeply notched
- Large head
- Barbel absent

10 cm

Length: 70–100 cm, up to 130 cm
Weight: 2–9 kg, up to 14 kg

A demersal species over the continental slope. Depth range: 200–1000 m, most common in 500–700 m. Spawning occurs during winter in the Westland coast, and during summer in the Chatham Islands.

Hoki *Macruronus novaezelandiae*

Maori name: Hoki

Silvery-blue

Long tapering tail

Second dorsal and anal fins: continuous with caudal fin

Skin delicate and smooth, mirror-like

10 cm

Length: 60–100 cm up to 130 cm
Weight: 1–3.5 kg up to 6 kg

A demersal species over the upper continental slope. Depth range: 150–1100 m, most common in 300–700 m. Spawning occurs during winter, mainly in the west coast of the South Island.

Ling *Genypterus blacodes*

Maori name: Hokarai

Mottled orange-pink and brown

Body long and rounded
Dorsal and anal fins continuous with caudal fin

Skin thick and smooth, body very slippery

10 cm

Pelvic fin barbel-like, below eye

Length: 80–120 cm, up to 160 cm
Weight: 4–10 kg, up to 20 kg

A demersal species over the continental shelf and slope. Depth range: 20–800 m, most common in 300–500 m. Spawning occurs during late winter and spring.

Garfish *Hyporhamphus ihi*

Maori name: Ihe

Lower jaw very long

Pectoral fin: short (shorter than head without bill)

10 cm

Length: 20–25 cm, up to 40 cm
Weight: less than 0.2 kg

A pelagic species on the continental shelf.
Depth range: 0–100 m.
Spawning occurs during early summer.

Saury *Scomberesox saurus*

Maori name: Karehe

Finlets: 4–6 pairs

Jaws elongated

10 cm

Length: 25–35 cm, up to 40 cm
Weight: less than 0.2 kg

A pelagic species in the open ocean. Occasionally over the outer continental shelf. Highly migratory.
Depth range: 0–200 m.

Orange roughy *Hoplostethus atlanticus*

Uniform orange after death
Large head with bony ridges

Dorsal fin: 15–18 soft rays

Belly: 19–25 small scutes

10 cm

Length: 30–40 cm, up to 60 cm
Weight: 0.8–1.6 kg, up to 3.5 kg

A demersal species on the middle continental slope.
Depth range: 750–1400 m, most common in 800–1000 m.
Spawning occurs during winter.

47

Alfonsinos *Beryx splendens* (Alfonsino); *Beryx decadactylus* (Imperador or long-finned beryx)

Body elongate (*B. splendens*) or body deep (*B. decadactylus*)

Dorsal fin: 4 spines, 13–15 soft rays (*B. splendens*); or 16–20 soft rays (*B. decadactylus*)

Dorsal fin base shorter than anal fin base

Anal fin: 4 spines

10 cm

Photo: *B. splendens*

Length: *B. splendens*: 30–50 cm, up to 70 cm; *B. decadactylus*: 30–50 cm, up to 100 cm
Weight: 0.5–1.5 kg up to 2.5 kg

A demersal species over the continental slope and seamounts. Depth range: 200–1300 m, most common in 250–400 m.

Similar common species

Red snapper (p. 49)

Rubyfish (p. 74)

Red snapper *Centroberyx affinis*

Maori name: Koarea

Bright orange-red with a silver-banded appearance because of bright scales

Dorsal fin: 7 spines

Dorsal fin base longer than anal fin base

Anal fin: 4 spines

10 cm

Length: 30–40 cm, up to 55 cm
Weight: 0.4–0.6 kg, up to 2 kg

A demersal species over the continental shelf and upper slope.
Depth range: 10–400 m, most common in 100–200 m.

Similar common species

Alfonsinos (p. 48)

Rubyfish (p. 74)

Lookdown dory *Cyttus traversi*

Pale brown above, silver on sides

Eye well up in the head

Dorsal and anal fin base lacking row of spiny scutes

Body rounded and very compressed
Pectoral fin: more than 14 soft rays

10 cm

Length: 25–40 cm, up to 55 cm
Weight: 0.5–1.2 kg, up to 2.5 kg

A demersal species over the upper continental slope.
Depth range: 200–1000 m, most common in 400–700 m.

Similar common species

Mirror dory (p. 52)

Silver dory (p. 53)

John dory *Zeus faber*

Maori name: Kuparu

Body oval and very compressed

10 cm

Olive brown with dark spot on side

Length: 30–40 cm, up to 65 cm
Weight: 0.8–1.5 kg, up to 3.5 kg

A demersal species over the continental shelf.
Depth range: 10–200 m, most common in 20–150 m.
Spawning occurs during summer with peak in February.

Mirror dory *Zenopsis nebulosus*

Silver with a faint grey spot on side

Dorsal and anal fin base with row of spiny scutes

Body almost oval (with pre-dorsal profile concave) and very compressed

10 cm

Length: 30–40 cm, up to 55 cm
Weight: 0.7–1.2 kg, up to 2.5 kg

A demersal species over the continental shelf and upper slope.
Depth range: 100–800 m, most common in 200–500 m.

Similar common species

Lookdown dory (p. 50)
Silver dory (p. 53)

Silver dory *Cyttus novaezelandiae*

Silver with pink fins

Eye in normal position (compare to Lookdown dory)

Dorsal and anal fin base lacking row of spiny scutes

Body almost oval and very compressed
Pectoral fin: less than 14 soft rays

10 cm

Length: 20–30 cm, up to 40 cm
Weight: 0.5–1 kg

A demersal species over the upper continental slope.
Depth range: 200–400 m.

Similar common species

Lookdown dory (p. 50)

Mirror dory (p. 52)

Black oreo *Allocyttus niger*

Body compressed
Large eyes

Profile slightly concave, not rising steeply

Second spine much longer than first spine

Dark brown

Usually one row of bony plates

Length: 25–35 cm, up o 45 cm
Weight: 0.5–1 kg, up to 2 kg

A demersal species over the continental slope.
Depth range: 400–1600 m, most common in 750–1200 m.

Similar common species (p. 55–57)

Oreos (Photo: Spiky oreo)

Smooth oreo *Pseudocyttus maculatus*

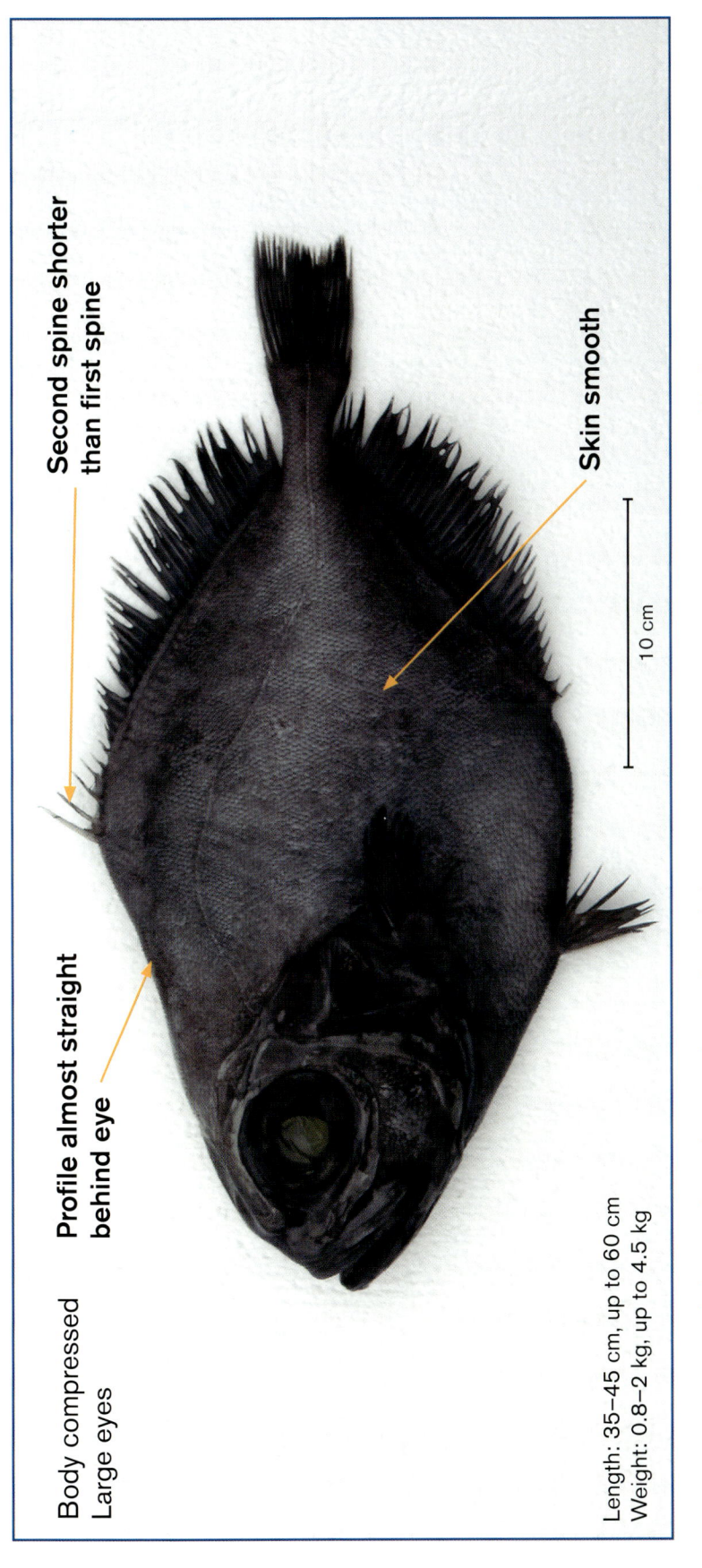

Body compressed
Large eyes

Profile almost straight behind eye

Second spine shorter than first spine

Skin smooth

10 cm

Length: 35–45 cm, up to 60 cm
Weight: 0.8–2 kg, up to 4.5 kg

A demersal species over the continental slope. Depth range: 650–1500 m, most common in 850–1100 m.

Similar common species (p. 54, 56–57)

Oreos (Photo: Black oreo)

Spiky oreo *Neocyttus rhomboidalis*

Body compressed
Large eyes

Profile very concave, rising steeply

Second spine much longer than first spine

Silver-grey

10 cm

Length: 25–35 cm, up to 45 cm
Weight: 0.8–1.5 kg, up to 2 kg

A demersal species over the continental slope. Depth range: 400–1250 m, most common in 500–1000 m.

Similar common species

Oreos (Photo: Black oreo) (p. 54–55, 57)

Warty oreo *Allocyttus verrucosus*

Body compressed
Large eyes

Profile not rising steeply, slightly concave

Second spine much longer than first spine

Dark brown

Two rows of bony plates

10 cm

Length: 20–35 cm, up to 45 cm
Weight: 0.5–1 kg, up to 2 kg

A demersal species over the continental slope.
Depth range: 1000–1600 m.

Similar common species

Oreos (Photo: Black oreo) (p. 54–56)

57

Sea perches
Helicolenus percoides (Scarpee)
Helicolenus sp. (Deepwater perch)

Maori name: Pohuiakaroa

H. percoides

Smooth bony ridge beneath eye without spines

Dorsal fin: 12 spines

Extensive variation of colour, from yellow-pink to dark red, brown and green. Scarpee present dark broad vertical bands

Photo: *Helicolenus sp.*

10 cm

Length: 20–35 cm, up to 40 cm
Weight: 0.4–0.6 kg, up to 1 kg

A demersal species over the inner continental shelf (scarpee) and upper continental slope (deepwater perch).
Depth range: 0–50 m (scarpee)/200–600 m (deepwater perch).
Ovoviviparous. Spawning occurs from early winter to late summer.

Similar common species

Scorpionfishes (p. 59)
Orange perch (p. 65)

Scorpionfishes
Scorpaena cardinalis (Red rock cod or Grandfather hapuku)
Scorpaena papillosus (Dwarf scorpionfish)

Maori name:
Matuawhaapuku (*S. cardinalis*)

Top of the head; *S. cardinalis*: one row of spines behind eyes; *S. papillosus*: or two rows of spines

Bony ridge beneath eye with spines

Dorsal fin: 12 spines

Length: *S. papillosus*: 10–20 cm, up to 25 cm; *S. cardinalis*: 25–35 cm up to 55 cm
Weight: 0.2–0.8 kg up to 1.4 kg

A demersal species over the continental shelf. Depth range: 0–200 m; red rock cod generally in deeper water than dwarf scorpionfish. Ovoviviparous.

Red rock cod   Dwarf scorpionfish

Photo: *S. cardinalis*

Similar common species

Sea perches (p. 58)

Red gurnard *Chelidonichthys kumu*

Maori name: Kumukumu

Red-pinkish above, white below

Snout without spines

Second dorsal fin base has row of spines

10 cm

Length: 25–35 cm, up to 60 cm
Weight: 0.5-1.4 kg, up to 2 kg

A bottom-living species on the soft bottom, mainly on the inner continental shelf.
Depth range: 20-180 m, most common in 20–100 m.
Spawning occurs during spring and summer.

Similar common species

Spotted gurnard (p. 61)

Spotted gurnard *Pterygotrigla picta*

Pink and yellow above, white below; all covered with black spots

Snout: two spines

Length: 20–30 cm, up to 40 cm
Weight: 0.5–1.2 kg, up to 1.5 kg

10 cm

A bottom-living species on the soft bottom, mainly on the outer continental shelf and upper slope.
Depth range: 60–400 m, most common in 150–250 m.

Similar common species

Red gurnard (p. 60)

61

Hapuku *Polyprion oxygeneios*

Maori name: Haapuku

Body slender
Gill cover has horizontal ridge ending in a spine

Dark blue-grey above, clearly distinct from pale sides and belly

Head pointed

Length: 70–90 cm, up to 150 cm
Weight: 5–20 kg, up to 40 kg

10 cm

A demersal species over the continental shelf and upper slope. Depth range: 5–500 m, most common in 100–400 m. Spawning occurs during winter.

Similar common species

Bass (p. 63)

Bass *Polyprion americanus*

Maori name: Moeone

Body deep
Gill cover has horizontal ridge ending in a spine

Uniform dark-grey

Head rounded

10 cm

Length: 70–100 cm, up to 180 cm
Weight: 5–30 kg, up to 100 kg

A demersal species over the continental shelf and slope. Depth range: 50–800 m, most common in 50–600 m. Spawning occurs during winter.

Similar common species

Hapuku  (p. 62)

Butterfly perch *Caesioperca lepidoptera*

Maori name: Oia

Tail lunate

One large black blotch and many small black spots

10 cm

Gill cover: three flat spines

Length: 15–25 cm, up to 30 cm
Weight: 0.3–0.5 kg, up to 0.8 kg

A demersal species over the continental shelf.
Depth range: 10–200 m.
Spawning occurs during winter and early spring.

Similar common species

Orange perch (p. 65)

Pink maomao (p. 66)

Orange perch *Lepidoperca aurantia*

Gill cover: three flat spines

Red-orange with one large dark blotch on sides

Tail truncate

Anal fin: eight soft rays

10 cm

Length: 20–25 cm, up to 35 cm
Weight: 0.3–0.5 kg, up to 0.8 kg

A demersal species over the outer continental shelf and upper slope. Depth range: 150–400 m. Spawning occurs probably during winter.

Similar common species

Sea perch (p. 58)
Butterfly perch (p. 64)
Pink maomao (p. 66)

65

Pink maomao *Caprodon longimanus*

Maori name: Maataataa

Pink reddish, mature males yellowish with a very large black blotch on rear of dorsal fin

Gill cover: three flat spines

Mature male

Tail slightly forked

Anal fin: three spines and eight soft rays

10 cm

Length: 30–40 cm, up to 55 cm
Weight: 0.5–1 kg, up to 1.6 kg

A demersal species over the inner continental shelf.
Depth range: 0–80 m.
Spawning occurs probably during winter.

Similar common species

Sea perch (p. 58)   Orange perch (p. 65)

Butterfly perch (p. 64)

Trevally *Pseudocaranx dentex*

Maori name: Araara

Lateral line: scute-like scales on posterior section

Finlets absent

10 cm

Body deep and compressed

Length: 35–50 cm, up to 70 cm
Weight: 0.4–2.0 kg, up to 5 kg

A mainly pelagic species over the continental shelf.
Depth range: 0–100 m.
Spawning occurs during summer.

67

Yellowtail kingfish *Seriola lalandi*

Maori name: Haku

Yellow fins

Bluish-green above, yellow stripe on sides; silvery-white below

10 cm

Length: 80–110 cm, up to 160 cm
Weight: 5–15 kg, up to 60 kg

A pelagic species in coastal waters.
Depth range: 0–50 m.
Spawning occurs during late spring and summer.

Jack mackerels
Trachurus novaezelandiae; Trachurus declivis; Trachurus murphyi

Maori name: Hauture

Secondary upper lateral line: present; *T. novaezelandiae*: just reaches the second dorsal-fin origin; *T. declivis*: well past second dorsal-fin origin

Lateral line: covered entirely by scute-like scales.
T. novaezelandiae (67–79) usually fewer than 76 scutes; *T. declivis* (73–89) usually more than 80 scutes; *T. murphyi* more than 90 scutes

No finlets

10 cm

Length: *T. novaezelandiae*: 15–35 cm, up to 40 cm; *T. declivis*: 20–45 cm, up to 55 cm; *T. murphyi*: 40–55 cm; up to 65 cm
Weight: 0.2–0.8 kg up to 1.5 kg

A pelagic species over the continental shelf and slope.
Depth range: 0–300 m.
Spawning occurs during late spring and summer.

Similar common species

Koheru (p. 70)

Blue mackerel (p. 104)

69

Koheru *Decapterus koheru*

Maori name: Kooheru

Body fusiform

Dorsal fin: 29 soft rays

Modified scales only on posterior part of lateral line

Finlets: one pair

10 cm

Length: 25–35 cm, up to 50 cm
Weight: 0.4–0.6 kg, up to 1 kg

A pelagic species in coastal waters.
Depth range: 0–100 m.
Spawning occurs during summer.

Similar common species

Jack mackerels (p. 69)
Blue mackerel (p. 104)

Kahawai *Arripis trutta*

Maori name: Kahawai

Dorsal fin: notch between spinous and soft sections

Caudal fin moderate size, upper lobe length less than or equal to head length

10 cm

Length: 40–50 cm, up to 65 cm
Weight: 2–3 kg, up to 5 kg

A pelagic species in coastal waters.
Depth range: 0–50 m.
Spawning occurs during summer; spawn earlier in the north than in the south.

Ray's breams *Brama brama; Brama australis; Xenobrama microlepis*

Head profile: blunt head in *B. brama*; sloping head in *B. australis* and *X. microlepis*

Body deep, almost oval, compressed

Dorsal and anal fins: stiff and erect; without anterior lobes curved

Upper lip fused with snout in *B. brama* and *B. australis*; free from snout in *X. microlepis*

Length: 35–50 cm, up to 60 cm
Weight: 1–2 kg, up to 3 kg

10 cm

A pelagic species in open ocean.
Depth range: 0–200 m.

Similar common species

Big-scale pomfret (p. 73)

Big-scale pomfret *Taractichthys longipinnis*

Body deep, almost oval and compressed

Dorsal and anal fins stiff and erect, long and curved anterior lobes

Large scales

10 cm

Length: 50–70 cm, up to 120 cm
Weight: 5–10 kg, up to 45 kg

A pelagic species in open ocean.
Depth range: 0–200 m.

Similar common species

Ray's breams (p. 72)

Rubyfish *Plagiogeneion rubiginosum*

Dorsal fin: 12 spines

Dorsal fin base longer than anal fin base

Caudal fin deeply forked

Mouth protrusible with scaled upper jaw

Length: 25–40 cm, up to 60 cm
Weight: 0.4–0.6 kg, up to 3 kg

10 cm

A demersal and pelagic species over the outer continental shelf and upper slope.
Depth range: 100–600 m, most common in 200–500 m.

Similar common species

Alfonsinos (p. 48)

Red snapper (p. 49)

Redbait *Emmelichthys nitidus*

Body fusiform

Very short spines at rear of spinous section

Broad pink stripe on sides

10 cm

Mouth protrusible

Length: 20–34 cm, up to 40 cm
Weight: 0.1–0.3 kg, up to 0.4 kg

A pelagic species over the continental shelf and slope.
Depth range: 20–300 m.

Red mullet *Upeneichthys lineatus*

Maori name: Aahuruhuru

Pink with blue and yellow areas

Profile of upper body more arched than lower body

Pair of long barbels

10 cm

Length: 25–30 cm, up to 40 cm
Weight: 0.4–0.6 kg, up to 0.8 kg

A demersal species over the inner continental shelf. Depth range: 0–100 m, most common in 0–50 m. Spawning occurs during spring and summer in pairs.

Snapper *Pagrus auratus*

Maori name: Tamure

Dorsal fin: 12 spines

10 cm

Length: 30–50 cm, up to 100 cm
Weight: 1–2.5 kg, up to 19 kg

A demersal species over the continental shelf.
Depth range: 5–200 m, most common in 5–100 m.
Spawning occurs during spring and summer, with activity peaking in November/December.

Giant boarfish *Paristiopterus labiosus*

Long snout and pre-dorsal profile rising steeply (adults)

Dark bands mostly present

Rough and bony head; small mouth

10 cm

Length: 45–60 cm, up to 85 cm
Weight: 1–2.5 kg, up to 12 kg

A demersal species on the continental shelf and slope.
Depth range: 10–260 m.
Spawning probably occurs during summer.

Southern boarfish *Pseudopentaceros richardsoni*

Dorsal fin: 14–15 spines

Silver-blue above and silver below

Head with fine markings (exposed bones)

Small mouth

Length: 30–50 cm, up to 60 cm
Weight: 1–2 kg

10 cm

A pelagic species over the continental shelf and slope.
Depth range: 0–500 m.

Blue maomao *Scorpis violaceus*

Maori name: Maomao

Uniform violet after death

Dorsal fin: spinous section lower than soft rays section

10 cm

Length: 20–30 cm, up to 40 cm
Weight: 0.2–0.8 kg

Coastal species.
Depth range: 0–50 m.
Spawning occurs during winter.

Parore *Girella tricuspidata*

Maori name: Parore

Small head

Greyish-brown with dark narrow vertical bands

10 cm

Length: 25–45 cm, up to 60 cm
Weight: 0.4–1.2 kg, up to 4 kg

Coastal species.
Depth range: 0–50 m.
Spawning occurs during late spring and summer.

82

Tarakihi *Nemadactylus macropterus*

Maori name: Tarakihi

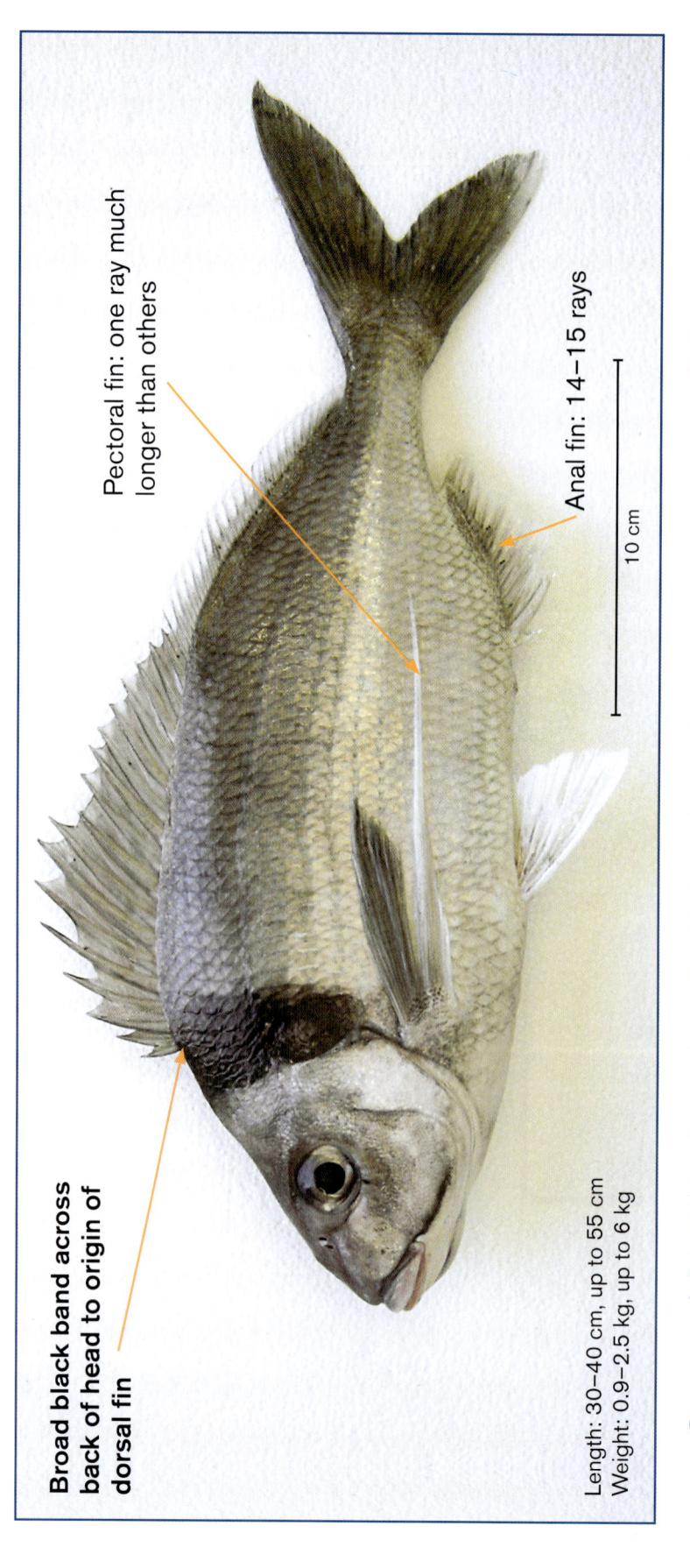

Broad black band across back of head to origin of dorsal fin

Pectoral fin: one ray much longer than others

Anal fin: 14–15 rays

10 cm

Length: 30–40 cm, up to 55 cm
Weight: 0.9–2.5 kg, up to 6 kg

A demersal species over the continental shelf and upper slope. Depth range: 50–350 m, most common in 100–250 m. Spawning occurs during summer and autumn, in offshore waters.

Similar common species

King tarakihi (p. 83)

Porae (p. 84)

King tarakihi *Nemadactylus* sp.

Broad black band across back of head to fourth dorsal fin spine

Pectoral fin: one ray much longer than others

Anal fin: 12–13 rays

Black tip on pectoral fin

10 cm

Length: 40–50 cm, up to 65 cm
Weight: 2–3 kg, up to 7 kg

Similar common species

Tarakihi (p. 82)
Porae (p. 84)

Depth range: beyond 50 m.

Porae *Nemadactylus douglasi*

Maori name: Porae

No broad black band across back of head

Pectoral fin: one ray much longer than others

Thick and rubbery lips

Length: 40–60 cm, up to 80 cm
Weight: 2–4 kg, up to 6 kg

A demersal species over the inner continental shelf.
Depth range: 10–100 m.
Spawning occurs during late summer and autumn.

Similar common species

Tarakihi (p. 82)

King tarakihi (p. 83)

Red moki *Cheilodactylus spectabilis*

Maori name: Nanua

Sides red-brown uniform or with several pale vertical bands some orange areas below.

Large and thick scales

Thick and rubbery lips

10 cm

Length: 35–50 cm, up to 70 cm
Weight: 1–1.8 kg, up to 4 kg

A demersal species on shallow, coastal and rocky reefs.
Depth range: 0–30 m.
Spawning occurs during autumn.

Blue moki *Latridopsis ciliaris*

Maori name: Moki

Dorsal fin: long, notched between spinous and soft sections

Thick and rubbery lips

Blue-grey above, lighter on sides; silvery below

Tail without black margin

Length: 50–70 cm, up to 90 cm
Weight: 2–2.5 kg, up to 10 kg

10 cm

A demersal species over the inner continental shelf.
Depth range: 10–100 m.
Spawning occurs during winter; they migrate to the only known spawning ground near East Cape.

Similar common species

Copper moki (p. 88)

Trumpeter *Latris lineata*

Maori name: Kohikohi

Dorsal fin: long, notched between spinous and soft sections

Three dark-green horizontal stripes on upper side

Thick and rubbery lips

Length: 60–70 cm, up to 110 cm
Weight: 4–7 kg, up to 15 kg

10 cm

A demersal species over the continental shelf.
Depth range: 10–200 m.
Spawning occurs during winter and early spring.

Similar common species

Copper moki (p. 88)

87

Copper moki *Latridopsis forsteri*

Dorsal fin: long, notched between spinous and soft sections

Body silvery with several thin pinkish-olive lines along the side

Tail with black margin

10 cm

Length: 30–60 cm, up to 70 cm
Weight: 1–2 kg, up to 4 kg

A demersal species over the inner continental shelf
Depth range: 10–100 m
Spawning occurs during winter

Similar common species

Blue moki (p. 86)

Wrasses Family *Labridae* (16 New Zealand species)

Body oblong to elongate

Usually very colourful. Most species can be identified by their colour pattern, even though coloration changes with the age and sex of the fish

Caudal fin mostly truncated or rounded

Small mouth

Large teeth at front of jaws

Length: 20–30 cm, up to 60 cm
(banded wrasse is the largest NZ wrasse species)
Weight: 0.3–0.8 kg, up to 2.5 kg

10 cm

Photo: *Pseudolabrus fucicola*

A demersal species in reefs on the continental shelf.
Depth range: 10–50 m.
Spawning occurs during different seasons for the different species; some in winter, others in summer.

Butterfish *Odax pullus*

Maori name: Mararii, Kooeaea

Small mouth with parrot-like teeth

Dark green-brownish after death

Scales small, more than 65 on lateral line

10 cm

Length: 30–50 cm, up to 70 cm
Weight: 1–1.5 kg, up to 2.5 kg

A demersal species in shallow waters.
Depth range: 0–20 m.
Spawning occurs during an extended period from mid winter to midsummer, with activity peaking in spring.

Grey mullet *Mugil cephalus*

Maori name: Kanae

Flattened, broad head

Dorsal fins widely separated

Anal fin: eight soft rays

10 cm

Lateral line absent

Eye pale yellow, with a transparent membrane

Length: 30–40 cm up to 60 cm
Weight: 0.5–1 kg up to 5 kg

A pelagic species in shallow waters and estuarine lagoons of rivers.
Depth range: 0–50 m.
Spawning occurs during late summer.

Similar common species

Yellow-eyed mullet (p. 92)

91

Yellow-eyed mullet *Aldrichetta forsteri*

Maori name: Aua

- Dorsal fins widely separated
- Anal fin: 12–13 soft rays
- Lateral line absent
- 10 cm
- **Head not flattened or broad**
- **Eye bright yellow, without a transparent membrane**

Length: 10–30 cm up to 40 cm
Weight: 0.3–0.5 kg up to 1 kg

A pelagic species in shallow and estuarine waters.
Depth range: 0–50 m.
Spawning occurs during summer and autumn.

Similar common species

Grey mullet (p. 91)

Blue cod *Parapercis colis*

Maori name: Raawaru

Rounded head

Dorsal fin: continuous with five short spines

Brown to blue-grey. Colour fades quickly after death

10 cm

Length: 30–40 cm, up to 60 cm
Weight: 0.8–1.5 kg, up to 3 kg

A demersal species in shallow coastal waters and over the inner continental shelf.
Depth range: 0–150 m.
Spawning occurs during spring.

Giant stargazer *Kathetostoma giganteum*

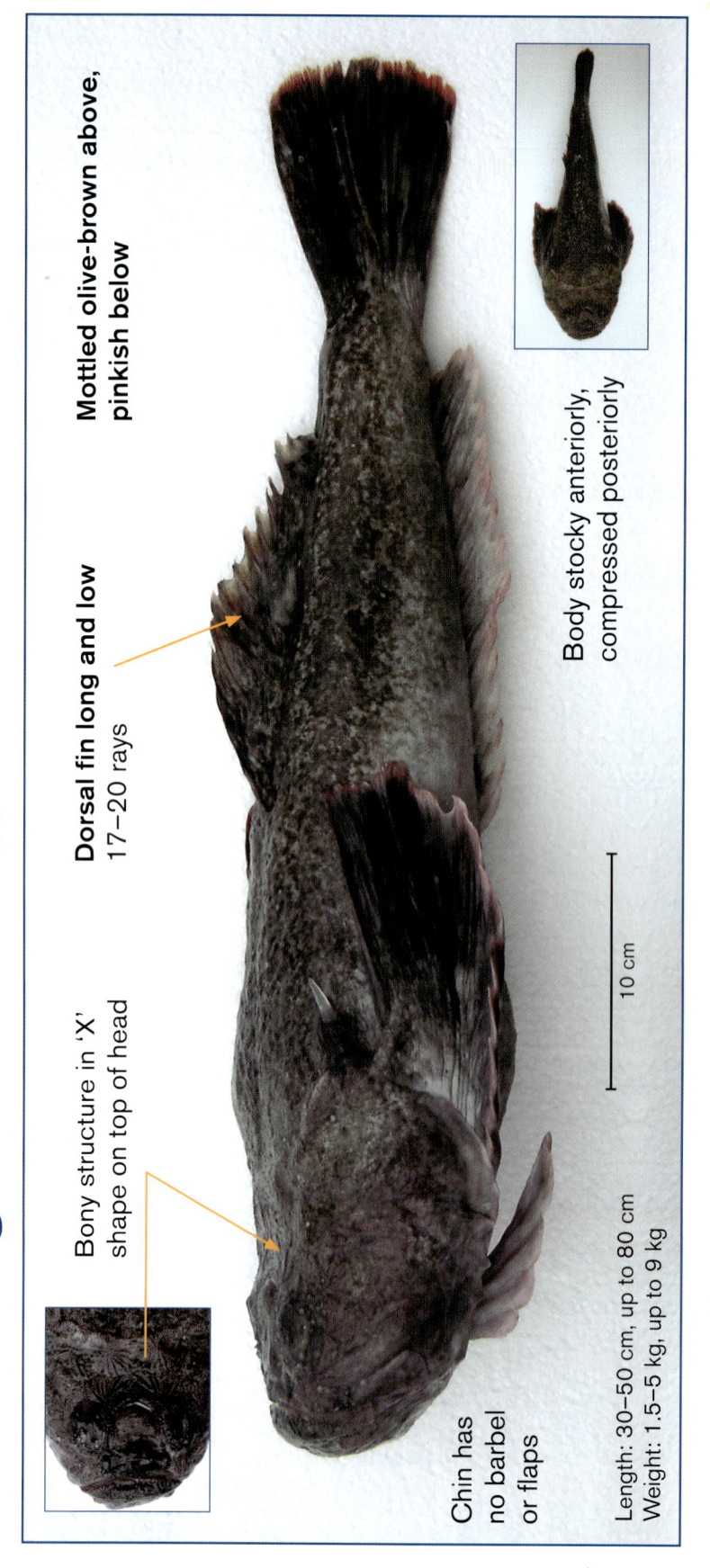

Bony structure in 'X' shape on top of head

Mottled olive-brown above, pinkish below

Dorsal fin long and low 17–20 rays

Body stocky anteriorly, compressed posteriorly

Chin has no barbel or flaps

Length: 30–50 cm, up to 80 cm
Weight: 1.5–5 kg, up to 9 kg

10 cm

A bottom-dwelling species on the continental shelf and upper slope.
Depth range: 50–600 m.
Spawning occurs during winter.

Similar common species (p. 95–98)

Stargazers (Photo: Banded giant stargazer)

Banded giant stargazer *Kathetostoma* sp.

No bony structure in 'X' shape on top of head

Chin has no barbel or flaps

Length: 25–45 cm, up to 60 cm
Weight: 0.5–2 kg, up to 5 kg

Dorsal fin short and high 14–16 rays

Body very stocky anteriorly, compressed posteriorly

10 cm

A bottom-dwelling species on the continental shelf and slope. Depth range: 50–300 m.

Similar common species

Stargazers (Photo: Giant stargazer)   (p. 94, 96–98)

Brown stargazer *Gnathagnus innotabilis*

Uniform brown above, pure white below

Body stocky anteriorly, compressed posteriorly

Scales clearly visible

Chin with two flaps

10 cm

Length: 30–40 cm, up to 60 cm
Weight: 0.8–2.5 kg, up to 5 kg

A bottom-dwelling species on the continental shelf.
Depth range: 0–200 m.

Similar common species

Stargazers (Photo: Giant stargazer)    (p. 94–95, 97–98)

Spotted stargazer *Genyagnus monopterygius*

Maori name: Kourepoua

Dark greenish-brown to grey with large pale spots

Body very stocky anteriorly, compressed posteriorly

10 cm

Chin with small barbel

Length: 20–30 cm up to 35 cm
Weight: 0.5–1.5 kg

A bottom-dwelling species on the continental shelf.
Depth range: 0–200 m.
Spawning occurs in spring and early summer.

Similar common species

Stargazers (Photo: Giant stargazer)  (p. 94–96, 98)

Scaly stargazer *Pleuroscopus pseudodorsalis*

Mottled dark bluish-grey

Dorsal fin preceded by several short spines or protuberances

Large, firm scales

Body very stocky anteriorly, compressed posteriorly

10 cm

Length: 50–60 cm at least, up to 85 cm
Weight: at least up to 13 kg

A bottom-dwelling species on the continental slope.
Depth range: beyond 600 m.

Similar common species

Stargazers (Photo: Giant stargazer)  (p. 94–97)

Barracouta *Thyrsites atun*

Maori name: Mangaa

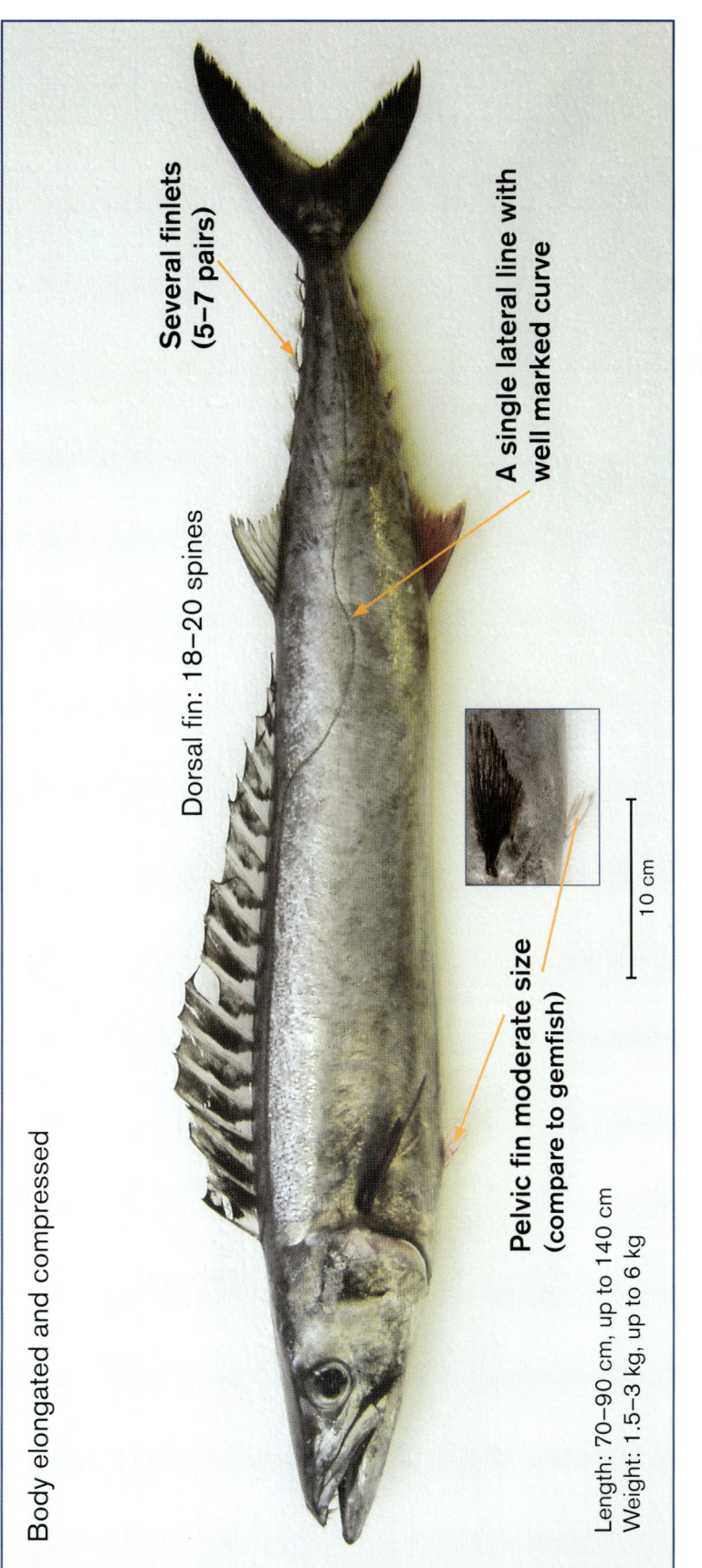

Body elongated and compressed

Several finlets (5–7 pairs)

A single lateral line with well marked curve

Dorsal fin: 18–20 spines

Pelvic fin moderate size (compare to gemfish)

10 cm

Length: 70–90 cm, up to 140 cm
Weight: 1.5–3 kg, up to 6 kg

A pelagic species over the continental shelf and sporadically on the slope. Depth range: 0–400m, most common in 50–200 m. Spawning occurs through most of the year, from late winter to autumn.

Similar common species

Gemfish (p. 100)

99

Gemfish *Rexea solandri*

Maori name: Tiikati

Body elongated and compressed

- A few finlets
- Double lateral line
- Pelvic fin very small

Length: 60–90 cm, up to 120 cm
Weight: 2–5 kg, up to 15 kg

A pelagic and demersal species over the outer continental shelf and upper slope.
Depth range: 100–800 m, most common in 150–400 m.

Similar common species

Barracouta (p. 99)

Oilfish *Ruvettus pretiosus*

Body elongated and compressed

Skin rough, covered with spiny scales

A few finlets

10 cm

Length: 80–150 cm, up to 300 cm
Weight: 6–20 kg, up to 100 kg

A pelagic species in open ocean.
Depth range: 100–700 m.

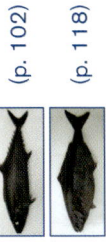

Similar common species

Escolar (p. 102)

Rudderfish (p. 118)

Escolar *Lepidocybium flavobrunneum*

Lateral line undulating

One large keel, flanked by two smaller keels

Several finlets

Length: 80–120 cm, up to 200 cm
Weight: 6–15 kg, up to 45 kg

A pelagic species in the open ocean
Depth range: 100–300 m

Similar common species

Oilfish (p. 101)

Rudderfish (p. 118)

Frostfish *Lepidopus caudatus*

Maori name: Paara

Uniform bright silver
Body very long and extremely compressed

Head with a crest

Caudal fin very small

10 cm

Length: 120–140 cm, up to 160 cm
Weight: 1.5–2.5 kg, up to 6 kg

A demersal and pelagic species over the upper continental slope.
Depth range: 200–600 m, most common in 300–400 m.

Blue mackerel *Scomber australasicus*

Maori name: Tawatawa

Blue-green above with an irridescent sheen
Wavy, dark lines on back

Several finlets

No modified scales on the lateral line

10 cm

Length: 30–40 cm, up to 55 cm
Weight: 0.4–1 kg, up to 1.5 kg

A pelagic species over the continental shelf
Depth range: 0–400 m, most common in 0–150 m
Spawning occurs in summer

Similar common species

Jack mackerels (p. 69)

Koheru (p. 70)

Butterfly tuna *Gasterochisma melampus*

Rounded head

First dorsal fin: depressible into grooves

Caudal fin: lunate

Very large scales

10 cm

Length: up to 200 cm
Weight: 20–60 kg

Depth range: 0–200 m.

Albacore *Thunnus alalunga*

First dorsal fin depressible into grooves

Tail with a white posterior margin

Pectoral fin very long, extended well past second dorsal fin

Anal finlets without yellow

Length: 50–70 cm, up to 100 cm
Weight: 3–10 kg, up to 55 kg

A pelagic species in open ocean. Highly migratory.
Depth range: 0–380 m.
Spawning occurs in the tropical Pacific; albacore reaching New Zealand for first time are probably 2–5 years old.

Similar common species (p. 105, 107–110)

Tunas (Photo: Bigeye tuna)

Skipjack tuna *Katsuwonus pelamis*

First dorsal fin depressible into grooves

Three to five dark horizontal stripes

Anal finlets dark, without yellow

Pectoral fin very short

Length: 45–60 cm, up to 70 cm
Weight: 2–5 kg, up to 8 kg

A pelagic species in open ocean. Migratory.
Depth range: 0–260 m.

Similar common species (p. 105–106, 108–110)

Tunas (Photo: Bigeye tuna)

Bluefin tunas *Thunnus maccoyii* (Southern bluefin tuna); *Thunnus orientalis* (Pacific bluefin tuna)

Dorsal anterior end of body cavity with a prominent muscular protuding 'bust' in southern bluefin tuna; without in Pacific bluefin tuna

First dorsal fin depressible into grooves

Keel: usually yellow but may become darker in large fish in *T. maccoyii*; dark in *T. orientalis*

Finlets yellow with black margin

Pectoral fin short; not reaching space between dorsal fins

Similar common species

Tunas (Photo: Bigeye tuna) (p. 105–107, 109–110)

Thunnus maccoyii

Thunnus orientalis

Length: *T. maccoyii*: 100–170 cm, up to 210 cm;
T. orientalis: 120–250 cm, up to 300 cm
Weight: 30–100 kg up to 200 kg

A pelagic species in open ocean. Highly migratory.
Depth range: 0–100 m.
Spawning: *T. maccoyii* occurs in northwest of Australia; fish reaching New Zealand for first time are five years old or more.

Yellowfin tuna *Thunnus albacares*

First dorsal fin depressible into grooves

Fins very long

Finlets bright yellow

Pectoral fin moderate, just reaching second dorsal fin

10 cm
Length: 60–120 cm, up to 200 cm
Weight: 20–80 kg, up to 170 kg

A pelagic species in open ocean. Highly migratory.
Depth range: 0–250 m, most common in 0–100 m.

Similar common species (p. 105–108, 110)

Tunas (Photo: Bigeye tuna)

Bigeye tuna *Thunnus obesus*

First dorsal fin depressible into grooves

Finlets yellow with black margin

Pectoral fin moderate, not reaching to end of second dorsal fin

Length: 100–160 cm, up to 220 cm
Weight: 30–100 kg, up to 200 kg

A pelagic species in open ocean. Highly migratory.
Depth range: 0–250 m

Similar common species

Tunas (Photo: Bluefin tuna)　(p. 105–109)

Broadbill swordfish *Xiphias gladius*

Maori name: Paea

Dorsal fin high and short in adults

Caudal peduncle: one large keel on each side

No pelvic fin

Bill very long and flat

10 cm

Length: 200–300 cm, up to 450 cm
Weight: 100–300 kg, up to 540 kg

A pelagic species in the open ocean.
Depth range: 0–550 m.

111

Dolphinfish *Coryphaena hippurus*

Dorsal fin starts above head

Hump headed

Blue-green above, usually yellow-green with peppering of black spots on sides

10 cm

Length: 70–100 cm, up to 160 cm
Weight: 6–10 kg

A pelagic species over the outer continental shelf and open ocean. Depth range: 0–85 m.

Blue warehou *Seriolella brama*

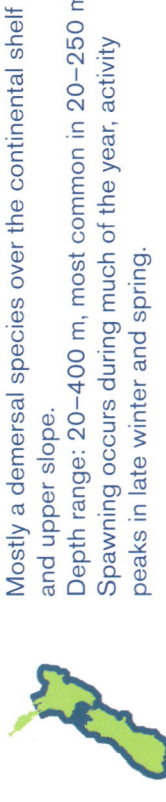

Maori name: Warehou

Scaleless patch truncated posteriorly on rear of head

Dorsal fin: 25–29 soft rays

10 cm

Long pectoral fin

Large dark blotch

Length: 40–55 cm, up to 70 cm
Weight: 1–3 kg, up to 7 kg

Mostly a demersal species over the continental shelf and upper slope.
Depth range: 20–400 m, most common in 20–250 m. Spawning occurs during much of the year, activity peaks in late winter and spring.

Similar common species

Silver warehou (p. 114)
White warehou (p. 115)
Ocean blue-eye (p. 116)

Silver warehou *Seriolella punctata*

Dorsal fin: 35–39 soft rays

Scaleless patch pointed posteriorly (dark 'V') at rear of head

Large dark blotch

10 cm

Length: 40–55 cm, up to 70 cm
Weight: 0.5–2 kg, up to 5 kg

Mostly a demersal species over the outer continental shelf and upper slope.
Depth range: 50–650 m, most common in 200–500 m.

Similar common species

Blue warehou  (p. 113)
White warehou  (p. 115)

White warehou *Seriolella caerulea*

No dark patch above pectoral fin base

Dorsal fin: 30–33 soft rays

10 cm

Length: 45–55 cm, up to 70 cm
Weight: 1–3 kg, up to 6 kg

A demersal species over the continental slope. Depth range: 200–800 m, most common in 400–700 m. Spawning occurs during late winter and spring.

Similar common species

Blue warehou (p. 113)
Silver warehou (p. 114)

Ocean blue-eye *Schedophilus labyrinthicus*

Poorly developed spinous section

Dorsal fin: 26–29 soft rays

Rounded snout

No dark blotch

Length: 55–80 cm up to 100 cm
Weight: 2–10 kg up to 50 kg

A benthopelagic species above rocky bottom and seamounts.
Depth range: 100–400 m.

Similar common species

Blue warehou (p. 113)

Bluenose (p. 117)

Bluenose *Hyperoglyphe antarctica*

Maori name: Matiri

Blunt snout and large eye

Short spines but well developed spinous section

Dorsal fin: 18–21 soft rays

Length: 60–100 cm, up to 130 cm
Weight: 2–10 kg, up to 50 kg

10 cm

A benthopelagic species above rocky bottom and seamounts. Depth range: 200–1000 m, most common in 300–700 m. Spawning occurs during winter.

Similar common species

Ocean blue-eye (p. 116)

117

Rudderfish *Centrolophus niger*

Body elongate and compressed

Blunt snout

Dorsal fin long and low, without spines

Finlets absent

10 cm

Length: 80–100 cm, up to 120 cm
Weight: 8–14 kg, up to 20 kg

A pelagic species in the open ocean.
Depth range: 300–700 m.

Similar common species

Oilfish (p. 101)

Escolar (p. 102)

Lemon sole *Pelotretis flavilatus*

Maori name: Paatiki

Dorsal-fin origin above eye

Body very flattened
Eyes on right side of head

Two fins on underside

Length: 25–35 cm, up to 50 cm
Weight: less than 0.8 kg

10 cm

A bottom-living species over the continental shelf.
Depth range: 0–200 m.
Spawning occurs during winter and spring in sheltered bays.

Similar common species

Flatfishes (Photo: Sand flounder)   (p. 120–125)

119

New Zealand sole

Peltorhamphus novaezelandiae

Maori name: Paatiki rori

Body very flattened
Eyes on right side of head

Long pectoral fin

Mouth on underside
Two fins on underside

Length: 25–40 cm, up to 55 cm
Weight: less than 0.8 kg

10 cm

A bottom-living species over the inner continental shelf.
Depth range: 0–100 m.
Spawning occurs during winter and spring.

Similar common species

Flatfishes (Photo: Sand flounder) (p. 119, 121–125)

Yellowbelly flounder *Rhombosolea leporine*

Maori name: Paatiki totara

Body very flattened
Eyes on right side of head

Underside yellow, peppered with white and dark spots
One fin on underside

Length: 25–40 cm, up to 50 cm
Weight: less than 0.8 kg

Oval body shape

10 cm

A bottom-living species in shallow waters.
Depth range: 0–50 m.
Spawning occurs during winter and spring.

Similar common species

Flatfishes (Photo: Sand flounder)   (p. 119–120, 122–125)

Sand flounder *Rhombosolea plebeia*

Maori name: Paatiki

Diamond body shape

Body very flattened
Eyes on right side of head

White underside, often with dark blotches
One fin on underside

Length: 25–35 cm, up to 45 cm
Weight: less than 0.8 kg

A bottom-living species on the inner continental shelf.
Depth range: 0–100 m.
Spawning occurs during a long period from autumn to spring.

Similar common species

Flatfishes (Photo: Yellowbelly flounder)   (p. 119–121, 123–125)

Greenback flounder *Rhombosolea tapirina*

Snout pointed and fleshy

Body very flattened
Eyes on right side of head

One fin on underside

Dark green (ocular side), white (underside)

Length: 25–40 cm, up to 50 cm
Weight: less than 0.8 kg

A bottom-living species in coastal waters.
Depth range: 0–100 m.
Spawning occurs during winter.

10 cm

Similar common species

Flatfishes (Photo: Sand flounder) (p. 119–122, 124–125)

Brill *Colistium guntheri*

Maori name: Paatiki nui

Short rostral hook

Body very flattened and oval
Eyes on right side of head

Colouration: regular pattern on ocular side

Two fins on underside

Length: 25–40 cm, up to 70 cm
Weight: 1.5–2.5 kg, up to 6 kg

A bottom-living species over the inner continental shelf.
Depth range: 0–100m, most common in 0–50 m.

Similar common species

Flatfishes (Photo: Sand flounder)    (p. 119–123, 125)

Turbot *Colistium nudipinnis*

Maori name: Paatiki

Body very flattened and oval
Eyes on right side of head

Long rostral hook

Two fins on underside

Length: 25–45 cm, up to 80 cm
Weight: 2–3 kg, up to 7 kg

A bottom-living species on the inner continental shelf.
Depth range: 0–100 m, most common 0–50 m.

Similar common species

Flatfishes (Photo: Sand flounder) (p. 119–124)

125

Leatherjacket *Parika scaber*

Maori name: Kookiri

Skin 'furry'

Fins yellowish

Pelvic fin absent

10 cm

Length: 20–25 cm, up to 30 cm
Weight: 0.2–0.5 kg

A demersal and pelagic species over the inner continental shelf. Depth range: 0–100 m, most common in 10–30 m. Spawning occurs during winter and spring.

Moonfish *Lampris guttatus*

**Silvery-blue with light spots.
Red fins**

Length: 80–130 cm, up to 180 cm
Weight: 20–50 kg, up to 270 kg

A pelagic species of the open ocean.
Depth range: 200–500 m.

|10 cm|

References

Anderson, O.F., Bagley, N.W., Hurst, R.J., Francis, M.P., Clark, M.R. and Mcmillan, P.J., 'Atlas Of New Zealand Fish And Squid Distributions from Research Bottom Trawls'. *NIWA Technical Report 42*, 1998.

Armitage, R.O., Payne, D.A., Lockley, G.J., Currie, H.M., Colban, R.L., Lamb, B.G. and Paul, L.J. 'Guide Book To New Zealand Commercial Fish Species.' New Zealand Fishing Industry Board, Wellington, 1985.

Ayling, T. and Cox, G. J., *Collins Guide to the Sea Fishes of New Zealand*. Collins, Auckland. Second edition, 1984.

Bagley, N.W., Anderson, O.F., Hurst, R.J., Francis, M.P., Taylor, P.R., Clark, M.R. and Paul, L.J., 'Atlas Of New Zealand Fish And Squid Distributions from Midwater Trawls, Tuna Longline Sets, and Aerial Sightings.' *NIWA Technical Report 72*, 2000.

Beentjes, M.P., 'Identification and Reporting of Commercial Skate Landings'. *New Zealand Fisheries Assessment Report No. 2005/16*. Ministry of Fisheries, Wellington, 2005.

Clement, I.T., Spear, T.H.A. and Paulin, C.D., *New Zealand Commercial Fisheries: The Guide to the Quota Management System*. Clement and Associates Limited and Oceanlaw New Zealand, Nelson, 2003.

Compagno, L. and Fowler, S., *Sharks of the World*. Princeton Field Guides, Princeton University Press, New Jersey, 2005.

Cousseau, M.B. and Perrota, R.G., *Peces marinos de Argentina*. Biología, distribución y pesca, INIDEP, Mar del Plata, 2000.

Crimp, D., *Hook, Line and Sinker: An essential guide to New Zealand fish*. HarperCollins Publishers, Auckland, 2003.

Doak, Wade, *A Photographic Guide to Sea Fishes of New Zealand*. New Holland Publishers, Auckland, 2003.

FIGIS – Fisheries global information syste. 2006 – FAO/SIDP Species Identification Sheet. http://www.fao.org

Fishbase 2006. Species Summary. http://www.fishbase.org

Fishserve 2006. Commercial Fisheries Services Limited. http://www.fishserve.co.nz/services/findspecies/

Francis, M., *Coastal fishes of New Zealand: an identification guide*. Reed Books, Auckland, third edition, 2001.

Francis, M., and Cox, G., *Sharks and Rays of New Zealand*. Canterbury University Press, Christchurch, 1997.

Graham, E., *Australian Marine Life: the Plants and Animals of Temperate Waters*. New Holland Publishers, Auckland, 2000.

Hurst, R.J., Bagley, N.W., Anderson, O.F., Francis, M.P., Griggs, L.H., Clark, M.R., Paul, L.J. and Taylor, P.R., 'Atlas of Juvenile and Adult Fish and Squid Distributions from Bottom and Midwater Trawls and Tuna Longlines in New Zealand Waters. *Niwa Technical Report 84,* 2000.

Kuiter, R. H., *Guide to the Sea Fishes of Australia*. New Holland Publishers, Auckland, second edition, 2002.
Last, P.R. and Stevens, J.D., *Sharks and Rays of Australia*. Csiro, Australia, 1994.
Ministry of Fisheries Te Tautiaki i nga Tini a Tangaroa, 2006. www.fish.govt.nz
National Aquatic Biodiversity Information System (NABIS), 2006. Ministry of Fisheries www.nabis.govt.nz
Paul, L. J., *New Zealand Fishes – Identification, Natural History and Fisheries*. Reed Books, Auckland, second edition, 2000.
Paul, L. and Heath, E., *Marine Fishes if New Zealand 1, shoreline and shallow seas*. Reed Books, Auckland, 1997.
——, *Marine Fishes Of New Zealand 2, deeper coastal and ocean waters*. Reed Books, Auckland,1997.
Paulin, C., *Common New Zealand Marine Fishes*. Canterbury University Press, Christchurch,1998.
——, *New Zealand Quota Species Identification*. Ministry of Agriculture and Fisheries, Wellington, 1987.
Paulin, C., Stewart, A., Roberts, C. and Mcmillan, P., *New Zealand Fish – a complete guide*. Te Papa Press, Wellington, reprinted 2001.
Paulin, C. and Roberts C., *The Rockpool Fishes of New Zealand*. Museum of New Zealand Te Papa Tongarewa, Wellington, 1992.
Yearsley, G.K., Last P.R. and Ward R.D. (eds), *Australian Seafood Handbook – an identification guide to domestic species*. Csiro, Melbourne, reprinted 2001.
——, *Australian Seafood Handbook – an identification guide to imported species*. Csiro, Melbourne, 2001.

Others New Zealand publications
- *Journal of the Royal Society of New Zealand*
- *New Zealand Journal of Zoology*
- *New Zealand Journal of Marine and Freshwater Research*
- *New Zealand Fisheries Technical Report* (MAF, then NIWA)
- *New Zealand Fisheries Assessment Research Document* (MAF, then NIWA, then MoF)
- *Fisheries Research Bulletin* (MAF)
- *Seafood New Zealand* (SeaFIC) – Museum Marine File
- *New Zealand Professional Fisherman*
- *New Zealand Fishing News*

Index of common names

Albacore   106
Alfonsino   48
Anchovy   34

Banded giant stargazer   95
Barracouta   99
Bass   63
Bigeye tuna   110
Big-scale pomfret   73
Black cardinal   37
Black oreo   54
Blue cod   93
Blue mackerel   104
Blue maomao   80
Blue moki   86
Blue shark   16
Blue warehou   113
Bluenose   117
Brill   124
Broadbill swordfish   111
Bronze whaler   17
Brown stargazer   96
Butterfish   90
Butterfly perch   64
Butterfly tuna   105

Conger eels   35
Copper moki   88

Dark ghost shark   28
Deepwater perch   58
Dolphinfish   112
Dwarf scorpionfish   59

Eagle ray   26
Elephantfish   27
Escolar   102

Frostfish   103

Garfish   45
Gemfish   100
Giant boarfish   78
Giant stargazer   94
Greenback flounder   123
Grey mullet   91

Hake   42
Hammerhead shark   19
Hapuku   62
Hoki   43

Imperador   48

Jack mackerels   69
John dory   51

Kahawai   71
King tarakihi   83
Koheru   70

Leatherjacket   126
Lemon sole   119
Ling   44
Lookdown dory   50

Mako shark   14
Mirror dory   52
Moonfish   127

New Zealand sole   120
Northern spiny dogfish   23

Ocean blue-eye   116
Oilfish   101
Orange perch   65
Orange roughy   47

Pacific bluefin tuna   108
Pale ghost shark   29
Parore   81
Pilchard   32
Pink maomao   66
Porae   84
Porbeagle shark   15

Ray's breams   72
Red cod   39
Red gurnard   60
Red moki   85
Red mullet   76
Red rock cod   59
Red snapper   49
Redbait   75
Ribaldo   41
Rig   21
Rough skate   24
Rubyfish   74
Rudderfish   118

Sand flounder   122
Saury   46
Scaly stargazer   98
Scarpee   58
School shark   20
Scorpionfishes   59
Sea perches   58
Silver dory   53

Silver warehou   114
Silverside   36
Skipjack tuna   107
Smooth oreo   55
Smooth skate   25
Snapper   77
Southern bastard cod   40
Southern blue whiting   38
Southern bluefin tuna   108
Southern boarfish   79
Spiky oreo   56
Spiny dogfish   22
Spotted gurnard   61
Spotted stargazer   97
Sprats   33

Tarakihi   82
Thresher shark   18
Trevally   67
Trumpeter   87
Turbot   125

Warty oreo   57
White warehou   115
Wrasses   89

Yellowbelly flounder   121
Yellow-eyed mullet   92
Yellowfin tuna   109
Yellowtail kingfish   68

Index of scientific names

Aldrichetta forsteri 92
Allocyttus niger 54
Allocyttus verrucosus 57
Alopias vulpinus 18
Argentina elongata 36
Arripis trutta 71

Beryx decadactylus 48
Beryx splendens 48
Brama australis 72
Brama brama 72

Caesioperca lepidoptera 64
Callorhinchus milii 27
Caprodon longimanus 66
Carcharhinus brachyurus 17
Centroberyx affinis 49
Centrolophus niger 118
Cheilodactylus spectabilis 85
Chelidonichthys kumu 60
Colistium guntheri 124
Colistium nudipinnis 125
Conger verreauxi 35
Conger wilsoni 35
Coryphaena hippurus 112
Cyttus novaezelandiae 53
Cyttus traversi 50

Decapterus koheru 70
Dipturus innominata 25
Dipturus nasutus 24

Emmelichthys nitidus 75
Engraulis australis 34
Epigonus telescopus 37
Galeorhinus australis 20
Gasterochisma melampus 105

Genyagnus monopterygius 97
Genypterus blacodes 44
Girella tricuspidata 81
Gnathagnus innotabilis 96

Helicolenus percoides 58
Helicolenus sp. 58
Hoplostethus atlanticus 47
Hydrolagus novaezelandiae 28
Hydrolagus sp. 29
Hyperoglyphe antarctica 117
Hyporhamphus ihi 45

Isurus oxyrinchus 14

Kathetostoma giganteum 94
Kathetostoma sp. 95
Katsuwonus pelamis 107

Labridae family (wrasses) 89
Lamna nasus 15
Lampris guttatus 127
Latridopsis ciliaris 86
Latridopsis forsteri 88
Latris lineata 87
Lepidocybium flavobrunneum 102
Lepidoperca aurantia 65
Lepidopus caudatus 103

Macruronus novaezelandiae 43
Merluccius australis 42
Micromesistius australis 38
Mora moro 41
Mugil cephalus 91
Mustelus lenticulatus 21
Myliobatis tenuicaudatus 26

Nemadactylus douglasi   84
Nemadactylus macropterus   82
Nemadactylus sp.   83
Neocyttus rhomboidalis   56

Odax pullus   90

Pagrus auratus   77
Parapercis colias   93
Parika scaber   126
Paristiopterus labiosus   78
Pelotretis flavilatus   119
Peltorhamphus novaezelandiae   120
Plagiogeneion rubiginosum   74
Pleuroscopus pseudodorsalis   98
Polyprion americanus   63
Polyprion oxygeneios   62
Prionace glauca   16
Pseudocaranx dentex   67
Pseudocyttus maculatus   55
Pseudopentaceros richardsoni   79
Pseudophycis barbata   40
Pseudophycis bachus   39
Pterygotrigla picta   61

Rexea solandri   100
Rhombosolea leporine   121
Rhombosolea plebeia   122
Rhombosolea tapirina   123
Ruvettus pretiosus   101

Sardinops neopilchardus   32
Schedophilus labyrinthicus   116
Scomber australasicus   104
Scomberesox saurus   46
Scorpaena cardinalis   59
Scorpaena papillosus   59

Scorpis violaceus   80
Seriola lalandi   68
Seriolella brama   113
Seriolella caerulea   115
Seriolella punctata   114
Sphyrna zygaena   19
Sprattus antipodum   33
Sprattus muelleri   33
Squalus acanthias   22
Squalus mitsukuri   23

Taractichthys longipinnis   73
Thunnus alalunga   106
Thunnus albacares   109
Thunnus maccoyii   108
Thunnus obesus   110
Thunnus orientalis   108
Thyrsites atun   99
Trachurus declivis   69
Trachurus murphyi   69
Trachurus novaezelandiae   69

Upeneichthys lineatus   76

Xenobrama microlepis   72
Xiphias gladius   111

Zenopsis nebulosus   52
Zeus faber   51

Acknowledgements

This guide has been made possible thanks to the logistic support of Simunovich Fisheries Limited, Sanford Limited and Auckland Fish Market. I would like to especially thank Vaughan Wilkinson for encouraging me to develop this project.

I am grateful to the fishermen and factory staff of the above companies for helping me to locate the fish specimens that were photographed, and also for sharing their practical knowledge on how to identify the different fish species. I am particularly grateful to Nenad Spiric, Patricio Pita, Ivan Vodanović ('Ćaruga') and skipper Andrew Gray.

Among the many people consulted I would like to thank the scientists of The Museum of New Zealand Te Papa Tongarewa and the National Institute of Water and Atmospheric Research (NIWA). Larry Paul gave me invaluable advice. They are not at all responsible, of course, for any inaccuracy in this guide.

Finally, the most heartfelt thanks go to dear friends and family who provided constructive suggestions. Thank you to Luis Colantoni, Adriana Aleksa and Fabiana Kubke.

About the Author

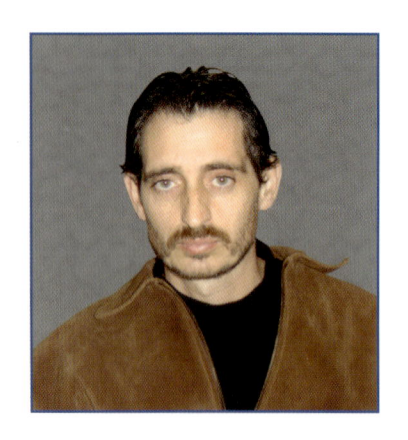

Born in Argentina, Jorge Hirt-Chabbert is a marine biologist who worked for several years in South America and the USA prior to settling in New Zealand. Much of his work deals with making research results accessible to non-scientists. Jorge has been involved in developing and implementing numerous programmes of science and technology for the private sector and government agencies. He is presently working as a fisheries consultant and researching the development of value-added seafood and marine products.
jhirtcha@gmail.com